Asmodeus
King of Daemons

David Thompson

King of Daemons
Asmodeus
High Magick Book 7

David Thompson

Trans Mundane
Publishing
Occult Knowledge

Copyright © 2023 David Thompson

All rights reserved.

Cover Photo: ID 109663849 © Vladimirs Poplavskis | Dreamstime.com

Trans-Mundane Press

Deluxe Hardback

ISBN: 9798218135492

To Fortuna,
Thanks for the warning

Introduction..1
  Need for Ritual..2
  CHAPTER ONE 5
  Possible Histories of Asmodeus 7
  CHAPTER TWO 10
    Hearing the Spirits 10
    The Pendulum 11
    The Tarot 11
    Ouija Board..12
    Other Divination Methods...13
    Making Contact..13
    Pronunciation Guide...15
    Preparations 16
    Your Altar...17
    The Rituals...19
    Magick Circle..22
  CHAPTER THREE..24
    King of the Daemons 24
      Money Manifesting 25
      Love and Lust Magick...26
      Knowledge 27
      Your Petition...27
      Sigils 28
    The Master King Asmodeus Ritual 30
    Pathworking King Asmodeus & Minor Daemon..................36
  CHAPTER FOUR...39
    King of the Jinn..39
      Your Petition...40
    Types of Jinn..41
    King of the Jinn Master Ritual 43
    Money-Specific JINN Ritual 49
    Love (Lust) JINN Ritual 55
  CHAPTER FIVE 61
    Hell's Banker 61
    The Draw Riches Ritual 63
    Pathworking Asmodeus as the Banker 67

- CHAPTER SIX 70
  - Asmodeus - Demon of Wrath 70
  - Wrath of Asmodeus Ritual 73
  - Wrath of Asmodeus Ritual Pathworking 77
- CHAPTER SEVEN 80
  - Master of Lust 80
  - The Draw Lust Ritual 81
  - The Draw Love Ritual 85
  - Pathworking the Lust Ritual 91
- CHAPTER EIGHT 93
  - Modifying Any Ritual 93
- CHAPTER NINE 95
  - The Sigils 95
    - Asmodeus Master Sigil 97
    - King of the Jinn Master Sigil 99
    - Hell's Banker Sigil 101
    - Asmodeus the Wrathful Sigil 103
    - King of Lust Sigil 105
    - King of Love Sigil 107
- Appendix 109
  - Recipes 109
    - Black Salt for Cursing 109
  - The Pendulum 111
    - Pendulum Charts 113
  - Suggestions and Links 116
  - Drawing the Pentacle while casting the circle 117
  - Color Correspondences in Magick 118
- About the Author 123

Introduction

Welcome to my book on Asmodeus

In this book, I'll examine a daemon who is number one all across the texts: Asmodeus. He also might be known as Ashmedai in your part of the word. He's a fascinating being, quite powerful, and he is King of the Jinn and King of the Demons.

I'll examine each aspect of Asmodeus, from his legacy of being the King to his energies as a wrathful entity, as well as his connection to money and gambling.

As I go over each aspect, you'll get the feeling Asmodeus is essentially a term for a collection of personalities of a "Daemonic" nature.

Is he just one being?

Like a lot of gods and goddesses, Asmodeus draws most of his personality and aspects of how people have used him in the past. Asmodeus goes back to the ancient times, being one of the daemons enslaved by Solomon to build the First Temple.

However, one must note here that stories found in many Hebrew texts are merely derivatives of the far older and more authoritative Sumerian cuneiform tablets. These Sumerian texts chronicled the religions and activities of the people of Sumer, considered the earliest known civilization on the planet (ignoring previous major civilizations, of course). Sumer existed as far back

6,000-7,000 years before present (B.P.).

After exploring the origins of Asmodeus, I'll then go over the various aspects, and how to contact each in a fairly simple set of rituals. I have taken the more archaic rituals, modified them and tested them, so that they will summon the aspect you intend to work with in ritual.

This book is a bit smaller than my previous books, but I get straight to the heart of the magick and then it's up to you, dear reader, to put this into practice.

I will also include "Pathworking" with each aspect, as it's proven to be effective in working the aspects of Asmodeus I present here.

Need for Ritual

In September of 2022, I found myself recovering from major surgery. I was stuck watching TV, and saw news of the death of Queen Elizabeth II. I later watched the queen's funeral. This was on the heels of my father's death and his funeral. Both had levels of ritual, with the queen's funeral so filled with traditional rituals it took them a week just to get through everything.

I came to the conclusion that humans need elaborate ritual in their lives. Many go to church less for the religion and more for the familiar rituals to connect to something larger than themselves.

However, many of us in this modern age feel like we can dispense with the more elaborate rituals and dive right into the core of any ritual, to appease a particular set of spirits, and have those spirits work for us.

High Magick lives for ritual. That's the very definition of High Magick!

Yet, in this series, I have simplified the traditional High Magick ceremony into much smaller rituals which can be performed by most anyone. My goal is to assist the reader in shifting their personal reality so that their (your) desires will manifest!

It may seem as if I am skipping important bits. Bits like "daemons are dangerous!" and the need to protect yourself. I had one reader of another book tell me I was giving dangerous advice when dealing with Daemons.

However, my methods of circle casting are such that a 99% majority of people working these rituals will not encounter any form of negativity, if you follow the precautions I specify in each ritual. If a being will not cooperate and perhaps you've done the ritual wrong, the most you can expect is nothing happening. That's right. The daemon will not suddenly possess you and begin making your life terrible.

With that said, the Law of Attraction will be in full force, in that what some people expect to have happen ***will happen***.

That's right. You will get what you expect. If your life is

terrible, it's possibly a result of your own pessimistic thoughts and habits. Many people blame others, including so-called "devils" for their own misery, when it's their own energies that draw to them misfortune.

When people caution about working with demons, tell scare stories about the bad things that could happen, they're unaware or unwilling to acknowledge that many of these spirits will fulfill those expectations. They are also aspects of our own energy. So, if you are a pessimistic, cautious person who expects these spirits to harm you, well, that will probably happen.

The need for ritual is all part of the acts we should perform to convince our own higher energy that we mean business, we really want this desire, and we're willing to prick a finger and bleed on a piece of paper to prove we actually mean it, this time for real, ***bring me my desire.***

Even while pathworking, make sure to take the time to make it a ritual, including the simpler self-protection visuals I will give you.

CHAPTER ONE

Why Asmodeus?

Spirits such as deities and so-called daemons seem to go to great lengths to get my attention and then ask for a book. Only one spirit *demanded* a book.

I was like, "Nope, not with that attitude." So, I ignored this spirit no matter what happened. Books flying off of shelves (one of the more annoying methods employed by my guide, Daniel, and other spirits).

When I say great lengths, I mean just that. Over the course of at least 8 weeks this past fall (2022), I had multiple people reach out to me and say that Asmodeus was reaching out to them, wanting my attention.

So, I gave in.

I did my usual research, digging deep into his past, plus channeling sessions where I attempted to make sense out of the recorded history and the spirits own version of this history.

Then, I entered a formal agreement, a pact, where I made damned sure he'd not only appear when summoned, but he'd also work on behalf of anyone using this book to summon him and present a petition. He had his own conditions as well, which are now all part of the rituals I will be presenting.

So, who is Asmodeus? He's a fascinating spirit. A spirit with a lot of history, quite a few mythologies mentioning him by his various names.

He has many, many names, including Asmoday, Osmodeus, Hashmedai, Shamdon, and occasionally Shidonai. In the Avestan (ancient Iran) language, his name means "wrath" and "daeva", or demon, thus "Wrathful Demon". It is through the Zoroastrian writings we first encounter a version of Asmodeus, as a wrathful daemon, and king of the Jinn!

He was enslaved by Solomon to lead the daemons who built the First Temple of Jerusalem. He is featured in multiple books of the Talmud, especially the Book of Solomon, where his enslavement by King Solomon is chronicled. According to the Talmud, Asmodeus was enslaved by Solomon using a ring given to him by Jehovah. Asmodeus was forced to assist in the design and building of the First Temple.

Asmodeus, like Lilith and scores of other deities, has multiple aspects:

King of Daemons - controlling lesser daemons

King of the Jinn - Control over the elusive Jinn

Asmodeus the Wrathful - Helps to speed up Karma

Prince of Lechery - personification of lust

Hell's Banker - Gambling and fortune magick

Each aspect has a slightly different way of summoning, and he gave me some interesting phrases to use. He has a traditional ENN, plus a few old seals/sigils used to summon him, but to my knowledge, no one has created anything new for Asmodeus since the 1960s, and these are based upon a single person's work with various daemons.

Possible Histories of Asmodeus

I label this section as "Possible Histories", because of the many, many sources of information on Asmodeus, the multiple translations of the texts, and the many, many false leads I encountered trying to get to the few kernels of truth regarding the King of the Daemons. Then this is combined with the energy and images I got directly from Asmodeus, himself.

Rabbinical and Hebrew texts were often taken from earlier texts (Example: Noah's Flood taken from the Story of Gilgamesh), I began researching those sources.

It is written that Asmodeus was tasked by King Solomon to assist in the building of the First Temple. It is written that Archangel Michael, on command from Jehovah, gave Solomon a ring with a magick seal that compelled the daemons to do as he commanded. Jehovah was big on slavery.

However, his name derives from a Persian term, Asmodai, which is at least 4,000 years old. Thus, Asmodeus appears to be one of the oldest spirits associated with the Goetia that I have encountered. In many cases, thousands of years prior to the oldest books of the Hebrew bible.

During a rather lengthy channeling session, I was given so much information, it's difficult to condense into one or two chapters. I have scenes of Asmodeus leading an uprising of other enslaved spirits against Solomon, thus fulfilling the prophecy of Solomon's reign being interrupted for many years. The uprising was ultimately unsuccessful, as texts indicate that Solomon returned to power and cursed Asmodeus, turning him into stone (or encasing him in stone).

Unlike the subjects of my other books, most of those spirits having been on the planet since previous civilizations, Asmodeus comes to us not as an Immortal Master, but as a powerful egregore based in Zoroastrian, Judeo-Islamic lore. Many, many ancient people believed in this Daemon of Wrath, and with the addition of more and more grimoires, Asmodeus' aspects emerged and grew more defined as the centuries went by.

He really hit the "big time" when he was included in the "*Malleus Maleficarum*", followed by "*Dictionnaire Infernal*", and of course, he's part of the Lesser Seals of Solomon as "Asmoday". Most of these texts were based upon older works, and pretty much describe the spirit as a King of Daemons, and only answering to Satan or Lucifer (depending on which text you are consulting).

Most texts have described his appearance as quite bizarre, more so than usual for daemons. Of course, texts which describe him in such wild forms might be to discourage neophytes from summoning him, or they were consuming a psychedelic substance. The Goetia describes him thus: He "is strong, powerful and appears with three heads; the first is like a bull, the second like a man, and the third like a ram; the tail of a serpent, and from his mouth issue flames of fire." Also, he sits upon an infernal dragon, holds a lance with a banner and, amongst the Legions of Amaymon, Asmoday governs seventy-two legions of inferior spirits.

Does sounds like someone who's had a bad night on some psychedelics and a strong cup of espresso.

In my experiences, if he manifests beyond simply being a presence in the room, it's usually as a large man with a silver crown. Sometimes in black, sometimes in light bluish-silver clothing. He is fond of disturbing the incense smoke, and like other spirits, he will often manifest within the smoke itself. This is why I always urge practitioners to use actual incense in a ritual. To do otherwise is missing out on a lot of the ritual, and possibly missing some interesting activity.

CHAPTER TWO

Hearing the Spirits

I am a medium.

My running joke is, they SAY I'm a medium, but my shirt tag says "Extra Large". It's an old George Carlin joke: "Edgar Casey was no medium; he was an extra-large."

Being a medium means I can hear spirits. I have worked for decades to not just hear the spirits, but to control when I hear them. It takes work to turn off the spirit radio. While writing this book, I would often lay down and close my eyes. The initial idea was to take a nap, but Asmodeus had other ideas. He'd appear in my mind, large, wearing a silver crown, and begin talking to me, what he wanted me to cover in this book. I'd send a thought back - "Now? Can't it wait?"

He must not be used to being told when and where he is allowed to communicate, as he usually would get angry.

But - I recognize that I am different from many practitioners, in that I can hear spirits once I have tuned in. Therefore, I now offer a special class that teaches how to hear spirits. It's part of my "Psychic 101 Course", available on my website. However, here I'll list the various ways one can attempt to hear a spirit communicate, and what methods might work best for you.

The Pendulum

This is my favorite. I just have to clear myself and make sure I'm not disturbed. All I need then is my amethyst pendulum (see appendix for detailed directions and product links) and a reading chart. I have furnished several for your own use, as well as blank answer charts.

A drawback of the pendulum is that is it especially sensitive to wishful thinking. This is even after clearing yourself. This has not only happened to me, but to several friends. I'd get messages online from one telling me their pendulum indicated that they're about to come into a large sum of money, and I'd caution them to temper their expectations.

The Tarot

Possibly the most accurate way to see what a spirit is trying to tell you. Most of the newer books are superior to the initial books I bought in the late 1970s. Choices were limited and that small, black cover paperback was damned hard to get through. My recommendations for a book are in the appendix.

I've been reading the cards for so long, I do not use any books any longer, unless I get nothing from the card. I find spirit can easily communicate with me via the cards, even when I don't feel as if I can tune into the issue and look ahead.

The tarot is simply a tool, and one we should all have in our toolbox.

Ouija Board

Outside of the tarot, I don't know of any other tool that is as misunderstood as the Spirit Board. It's not, in and of itself, evil. It's just a tool.

But it's a tool you need another person with you to actually get messages via the planchette. The best spirit boards are usually handmade, although I have used the mass-produced Ouija board quite effectively.

Aside from needing someone else, the other big drawback is how the board works. It appears that the planchette moves by itself, but it's actually our fingers making unconscious movements, which can propel the planchette across the board.

This doesn't mean I haven't used this to contact spirit. I have. Even when I was eleven and several friends were over and we decided to try it out. We scared ourselves silly using it. In my mind, there is no way the door blew shut and the lights flickered without the presence of a spirit.

Other Divination Methods

Crystal balls, scrying mirrors, black mirrors, tea leaves, all can be utilized to hear or fathom what the spirits are trying to say to you.

Though, honestly, all I have ever needed and used with any accuracy is the Tarot, and sometimes the pendulum. Your results may vary.

(Honestly, I was never, ever able to get the crystal ball or black mirror to work. I tried. I really tried.)

Making Contact

Like previous books, I advise the practitioner to make initial contact with the main aspect of Asmodeus before beginning work with any of the other aspects.

Working with the King, you will unlock access to hundreds, perhaps thousands, of lesser daemons and Jinn.

So let's dive in.

There is the time-honored method of using his daemonic ENN (think of an ENN as a sort of celestial telephone number), and after saying it three times, you then call to Asmodeus, imploring him to join with you, etc.

My method will make use of a special sigil, coupled with

a special phrase that originated in the earliest of texts and translated into our common language. Asmodeus gave me this phrase, so that you will get the correct aspect when you perform the ritual.

In only one ritual do we use Asmodeus' traditional ENN, but this is because that is the aspect we're calling upon.

In all but one instance, I will also present a method of pathworking, but I strongly advise you to establish a relationship with the King prior to calling on him in a pure mental ritual. Get to know him, and his appearance, so that you will know you have the correct aspect appearing when you do the pathworking.

The only aspect I do not present a pathworking for is Asmodeus as King of the Jinn. Here you will need to keep a traditional circle in order to successfully corral the elusive Jinn. Even with their King tasked to drag them to you, you still need the formality of the ritual to make this magick function as intended.

Yes, "intended." The Jinn are easily the most devious spirits I have encountered, and I have encountered plenty, including the legendary leprechaun. The Jinn have a motto, "Give the petitioner what they ask for, literally, and not what they actually want."

For example, you ask for much needed money, and unless you specify the currency in your corner of the world, they're liable to have you find a wallet of Central American currency. You got your money! But, it's practically worthless.

Traditionally, one would say the King's ENN three times, which acts as a cosmic telephone number. In this book, I'll be presenting new ENNs for King Asmodeus, which depend on the aspect you'll be summoning. For example, the Wrathful Demon I use the Sumer word for smite: Shargaz. I attempted to simplify the phrases, but Asmodeus really prefers the ancient tongues, and wants words of praise for his powers in each summoning. The original ENNs appear to be Germanic, but in most cases the phrases avoid direct translation.

Pronunciation Guide

In this book, I have multiple summoning phrases for King Asmodeus. While working the test rituals, pronouncing the phrases caused a bit of concern.

Although Asmodeus really doesn't care how the words are pronounced, I am including this short guide to how to say each phrase while in ritual.

These are in phonetic phrases, based upon the standard phonetics used in American English.

"**Sarrum Rabum ilu talamu Mahru**"
SAR-RUM RAH-BUM EELOO TALI-MOO MAH-ROO

"**Malik Al-jini Malik Allahab 'ana 'astadeik**"
MAH-LICK AL-GENNY MAH-LICK ALI-HEEB AH-

NAH AH-STA-DECK

> "Imum Shargaz Ankah Eh Mum"
> EYE-MUM SHA-AR-GAZ AANGK EH MUM

> "Lugal Ki Ta Lugal Hili"
> LOO-GAL KEY TAH LOO-GAL HIGH-LIE

> "Ayer avage aloren Asmodeus aken"
> AYE-YER AV-AGE AH-LOREN AZ-MO-DEUS AH-KIN

Preparations

Actually, precautions.

With Asmodeus, one has to be careful how you word your requests, and how you approach the King in general. Approach with respect, but don't grovel. Putting Asmodeus on a pedestal, elevating him above you, the magician, is begging for him to take advantage of you, draw upon your energy, and leave you wishing you'd never summoned this power being.

Cast a circle, if possible, and follow the traditional daemon circle casting. Asmodeus is a very traditional daemon, which means he's in the wish granting business, but usually looks for a way out. He can be dangerous. Not as dangerous as Sorath. In fact, I advise anyone thinking about summoning Sorath to choose another spirit.

Correctly wording your requests is really important. Unlike other spirits I've written about, Asmodeus, in some of his aspects, shouldn't be allowed to work without specific conditions. Conditions such as "by this weekend" can't work, but adding "being it to me safely, harming none" is a smart precaution for Asmodeus.

Your Altar

The King is a traditionalist. He likes it when you represent each element on your altar: Air (smoke), Fire (candle), Earth (crystals), and Water.

Each aspect has its own suggestions for candle colors and incense, but a basic set of white and black candles will always work. It's what I personally use. I will occasionally dedicate a single candle to a specific deity, such as red for Lilith, green for Fortuna, but I stick with white and black for most other deities and daemons.

Incense - almost anything is fine by the King. I will always use frankincense resin on a charcoal disc. Use a real incense, as the King doesn't appreciate using essential oils as you are missing the traditional "air" element of the ritual. Smoke equals air and has for millennia. Stick incense will also work. As long as it isn't too sweet.

For the offering, Asmodeus, in all his aspects, prefers a

drop of blood as a sacrifice.

Not animal blood.

Your blood.

So, you will need some sterile lancets and alcohol prep swabs. Do not use a household needle and stay away from using razor blades. You want a single drop of blood, you should not soak the sigil in a pool of your blood, no matter how badly you wish the manifestation to happen. As you increase the quantity of blood, it will not speed up the manifestation, nor will it make Asmodeus any more willing to work on your behalf. He's more likely to take advantage of this and ask for more, and more outlandish sacrifices. I have never had him request an animal, so don't even think about killing an animal for a ritual.

You will need a place to work, and you will need privacy.

You can work skyclad (e.g., nude) as Asmodeus loves a good show.

You can also use other bodily fluids as an offering, that's totally up to you. Sexual fluids make a good offering. Combine chaos, sex magick with a ritual to Asmodeus. He'll be quite happy. Like I said, he enjoys a good show.

It is completely up to you if you wish to make a semi-permanent altar to the King.

Magick ink is useful for writing petitions and pacts. It's not a very special ink, in fact I make "magick ink" once or twice a year. I take a small empty travel ink bottle (about 1 ounce, available online), I fill it with 1/2 oz of ink, then I poke a finger and add two or three drops of blood to this ink. I use a unique red fountain pen with this ink. Since blood thickens the ink, I find I have to dip the pen into the ink instead of filling it's reservoir, as the ink will tend to clog the pen's feed and then it's a pain to disassemble and clean, not to mention wasting the magick ink.

You can buy magick ink. I never have, not since learning of the fountain pen ink method. Plus, even with a low-end pen, fountain pen ink is really cheap and found at most stationary stores. Grab a Jinhao-branded pen online, and use it. I have ten of them, each ran me less than $9 to buy, including shipping.

The Rituals

Like my other books, I'll be using a basic ritual template, and adjusting each one to fit the aspect of King Asmodeus that we're going to summon.

In each ritual, the parts you speak are in **Bold** and occasionally in ***Bold Italic***, so it's easier to see when using this book in an active ritual. It's also good to practice a specific ritual, except actually burning the sigils, or petition. Simply make it your intent to do a "dry run", and not actually summon Asmodeus. If the King shows up, and you can hear his voice, ask him about how to best phrase your petition. He will assist you. I often work a base ritual to call upon any spirit so I can get feedback on a specific problem and how best to work the ritual.

Each ritual will specify what is needed, but there are some basic things you can get to use on your altar that will not vary from ritual type to another.

These items are the altar candles. Get some larger pillar candles, about 3 inches round by 3 inches tall. Make sure to have several white, black, and red candles, as these are the basic colors used in all rituals. I prefer a brand called "Mega Candles" and an internet search will bring up where you can buy them. Most any discount store will have white candles. The black is a bit harder to find, except during Halloween. Red is easy to source during the mid-winter holidays. Candles represent the element "Fire" in your ritual.

Incense is needed on an altar. You cannot use essential oils in a diffuser, as the incense smokes stands in for the element "Air", and is needed in any ritual to a traditional daemon like Asmodeus. He's pretty picky about having something soldering and emitting smoke on the altar. It can be a stick or cone incense, or resin on hot charcoal. I keep jars of frankincense resin in my temple area, as I use frankincense more than any other resin.

Incense blends are also appreciated. I got a sampler kit of resins, and I have made some blends which do quite well in ritual. I use frankincense as a base, after crushing it into small pieces, I then will mix small amounts of white copal, or dragon's blood into the base. A mix of copal, dragon's blood and sweet myrrh with frankincense seems to please most any deity or daemon I summon.

Don't over think using incense. Pick a blend, or go with pure frankincense. Hell, even a stick of Nag Champa will work for Asmodeus. Just don't try to use essential oils in a diffuser.

Altar cloth - I have two basic cloths. Both have black on one side with gold decoration on the other. When needing a solid black, I just reverse the cloth and that works. You might want to grab a red one, if you can find it. That works well with cursing rituals. Red is a color that typically means passion, and that emotion is needed when sending out a curse!

Miscellaneous items you will need for Asmodeus: Athame, useful for defining your circle and as a pointer when calling on the elements/direction guardians in the ritual. Crystals, which stand in for the "Earth" element. Goblet, for holding a small amount of water, which stands for the element "Water" (of course).

Placement of each item is totally up to you. There is no "correct" way to arrange your altar. I try to keep my altar to a minimum, as that is just how I do things.

Leave room for the sigil and fireproof bowl when arranging your altar, and make sure you have everything you need when it's time to begin the ritual. If you forget something, you will need to cast the circle again. After a few times, this gets tedious, so I have a check-list of things I need for a ritual, and I check each item off while preparing for a ritual. It can also be embarrassing, as I once had a daemon whisper "Dude, seriously? This is the second time you forgot something."

With the pathworking rituals, these are full mental, and should be done while in a light daydream state, also called "Alpha". Some are quite complex, and those typically walk you through the transition from our level of existence to the etheric plane where one can find a being like Asmodeus. He often has a gatekeeper, a smaller daemon who makes sure you are both ready, and worthy, of Asmodeus' time. In the standard ritual, you make the ENN callings and he will arrive, but the pathworkings do not have the ENN calls and operate differently. By setting up and working a full ritual, even a simplified ritual, shows Asmodeus you are serious in your intention, and he will arrive to listen to your petition.

This is no guarantee of Asmodeus actually working the magick on your behalf. You must also adhere to the necessities of each ritual, the blood sacrifice and the earnest desire for your petition be to acted upon, especially when it concerns wrathful magick. As with most of the spirits I include in a book, there's an agreement with them that they will attend to all requests that result from someone working these rituals.

Magick Circle

My basic use of a circle isn't protection, but to define the section of space/time that allows contact with spirits who mostly reside in the astral levels of our reality.

Sometimes, a proper circle can be skipped. *This isn't one of those times.*

With regards to this daemon, you absolutely must use a circle, as a way to control the demonic energies attracted by the magick used to summon Asmodeus. I give you a proper circle casting with each ritual. Even when pathworking, you need to protect yourself from stray daemonic presences.

Now, let's take a look at each aspect.

CHAPTER THREE

King of the Daemons

I work with multiple daemons each month. It's just what I do, to manifest my lifestyle, to manifest my future. I'm quite comfortable summoning spirits, even a powerful daemon like Sorath.

While working with minor daemons, it's often best to treat them with respect, which means to me, no binding or forcing the spirit into a "spirit house", or other container. There are practitioners who feel differently. While my approach works for many spirits, it doesn't work for them all. In those cases, call on King Asmodeus to make the lesser daemons live up to their end of the pact or agreement, which is agreed to while in ritual. (If you can't make contact and hear a spirit, see Chapter Two for ways to help hear the spirits.)

For this ritual, you will ask Asmodeus to call upon a minor

daemon, either of your own choosing, or allow the King to choose for you. It's better to have your mind on a specific minor daemon prior to summoning King Asmodeus. This way, you have a bit more control.

Some of these minor daemons are hard to deal with, and using Asmodeus to control them is one way of working with them. Since we do not have proper ENNs to summon some of these minor daemons, like the typical Goetia daemons, we need to use their King to make contact and have them appear to us in our circle.

The possible subjects for magick itself would fill a book, so I'll be brief. Of the basic subjects I have found most people wish to work on are Money and Love. Money because we need it in our modern society, you can't do a whole lot without money, but it's the most elusive energy to properly corral. This is a mindset issue, and several of these minor daemons also deal with gently rewiring your thought patterns to allow you to be more accepting of the flow of money/energy into your life.

You can create your own sigil or use the King Asmodeus master sigil and a smaller printout of the King Asmodeus Sigil.

Money Manifesting

The first daemon people think of associated with money is Bune. But there's a bunch, if you do any looking. Of the hundreds (if not thousands) of minor daemons with money as a power, you could try any of the following:

Nitika - possibly the most well-known minor daemon associated with money. She's the subject of several books, possibly originating with a late 1970s book by mystic Geof Grey-Cobb.

Shax - A goetic judeo-christian spirit associated with wealth - can be very tricky to work without Asmodeus' supervision. This one is one of the 72 demons used by Solomon.

Ala - Slavic. A class of female demons often subjugated by Asmodeus, and is good at finding hidden riches.

Caim - another Goetic daemon, one we hardly hear about, but is useful for drawing wealth to you, or uncovering sources of new income.

Laberzerin - Minor daemon last seen in a book by Geof Grey-Cobb, and is useful for assisting the practitioner with winning contests and lotteries.

Love and Lust Magick

I usually advise people to look at Aphrodite for love magick, and Lilith for Lust, however the King of Lust can assist as well, and I'll dive deeper into this magick in a later chapter.

Some minor daemons to use for love are:

Aamon - a goetic daemon, is a good one to use when you wish to find love. He also helps friends and family members reconcile.

Raum - another goetic daemon, good at pulling love to

you.

Saleos - another Goetic daemon, one who can pull men and women together in love.

Knowledge

Most entries of Goetia daemons have them answering questions, or imparting knowledge. This is because in the Middle Ages, most people were denied an education, with knowledge being considered a dangerous thing. So, of course, daemons would have taught mysterious knowledge as one of their powers.

Kadriel is a lower level angelic/daemon who is known to assist the magician in uncovering secret knowledge.

Stolas is a Goetic daemon who will happily answer your questions.

Your Petition

Once you have decided on a daemon, and you know what it is you want to manifest, it's time to but that all down on paper and begin the magick. The magick often begins to work while you are writing your petition.

The petition can be written in a variety of ways, and the best working is brief, simple, and with enough detail the daemon can't find a way out of delivering the desire.

This is just an example of a petition, how I would write

one to Nitika: *"King Asmodeus, I now ask that you bring Nitika, genius of wealth, into this circle, to listen to my petition. Nitika, you are a genius of wealth. I now ask that you fill my bank account with five thousand US dollars, by the next full moon. I ask that this money comes to me in a safe and harmless way. I thank you for listening, and I thank King Asmodeus for his kind assistance in this matter."*

This petition is a bit longer than I usually suggest, but it contains no way for a daemon to get the desire wrong. Such as the time I manifested money, found in a wallet on the street. Inside was a very large banknote from Costa Rica. But only worth a about a dollar in US currency once converted.

This petition would make for a messy sigil, but one can be made from such a long statement.

Sigils

For your specific petition, you will summon King Asmodeus, then ask him to escort the chosen daemon to your space to listen to your petition. Then you will present the petition to this daemon. Once this is done, you will be asked to give the sacrifice. For this, clean a finger with the alcohol prep swab, prick that finger and place a single drop of blood onto the smaller sigil.

Then the sigil is to be burned in the fireproof bowl, and the ashes stirred to make sure the sigil has burned completely. I use a long-handled tea-spoon for this purpose. I lift the edge of the paper, and allow the flames to fully consume the sigils.

If you made a sigil from your petition statement, you should activate it by passing it through the smoke of the incense, then ask King Asmodeus to bless the sigil. Then keep it on you, or hide it in your bedroom, such as in a clothing drawer or under a pillow.

The Master King Asmodeus Ritual

"Encouraging" a minor daemon to do your bidding

This ritual can, and should be, modified to accommodate ANY desire you wish to manifest.

Items Needed:

Black and White Altar Candles

The color needed for the desire (gold for money, red for revenge, pink for love)

Incense - frankincense or any other traditional incense

King Asmodeus' Master sigil

Crystals to represent Earth. Or some special (to you) rocks.

A goblet or wine glass of water

Small copy of the sigil for the sacrifice

Diabetic lancet

Fire-resistant bowl

Prepare your space

Arrange your altar in any way that suits you. Get the incense going. If using a charcoal puck, light it and allow it to become covered in ash.

Light all the candles (except for the candle for your desire).

Room lights out. Pay attention to this sequence. Candles, then the room lights out. Trust me, I've accidentally turned out the room lights, took a few steps and then cursed the darkness.

Prepare the ritual-specific candle for this ritual. I typically will place a drop of mineral oil onto the candle and coat it lightly. Then I secure it into a solid holder, as this candle should be burned completely after the ritual. Keep it in a safe place if you use a temporary altar.

Circle Casting

If you have the space, draw a circle on the floor with chalk. This will help define the perimeter of the sacred space. If not, don't worry. As long as you can define the circle using a crystal point, athame/dagger, or even your finger. Don't get overly attached to any one specific method of casting a circle. Not like some people who will insist you chant, or moan, and only walk in a specific direction. Trust me, the magick circle doesn't care how you define it, just define it.

Anyone who says differently should seek counseling, as they have issues.

I know I said this earlier, but do make sure you have everything will need in your space. Nothing can spoil the rhythm of a ritual like realizing you've forgotten the petition, or the gold candle, having to stop, then recast the circle. I can imagine the guardians looking at each other, some eye-rolls and slow head shaking. Especially Lucifer. He can roll his eyes into the back of his head, and grimace, then slowly shake his head. I know from experience.

Make sure you have everything will need in your space.

Define your circle, and then stand in the center. Stand with your right arm lifted, pointing in each direction as you summon the guardians. After saying each phrase, draw a simple pentacle in the air with a finger or wand:

Turn so that you are facing east and say:

"I now call upon the guardian of the east - Lucifer! Renich Tasa Uberaca Biasa Icar, Lucifer!"

Turn to the south and say:

"I now call upon the guardian of the south, Flereous! Ganic Tasa fubin, Flereous!"

Turn to the west and say:

"I now call upon the guardian of the west, Leviathan! Jedan Tasa hoet naca, Leviathan!"

Turn to the north and say:

"I now call upon the guardian of the north, Belial! Lirach tasa vefa welhc Belial!"

Finally, hold your arms up, and say to the sky: **"I now summon Satan, Ave Satanis! Satan, keep guard over this sacred space! This circle is sealed, and all unwanted and uninvited energies must depart my space now!"**

Main summoning:

Sit or stand facing your altar. Gaze upon the sigil. Then, summon King Asmodeus by saying the aspect-specific ENN three times:

> **Sarrum Rabum ilu talamu Mahru**
> **Sarrum Rabum ilu talamu Mahru**
> **Sarrum Rabum ilu talamu Mahru**
> **King Asmodeus, I now summon you!**
> **Join with me! Be with me in my space!**

Pause a few moments. At this point, look for any signs the King is nearby, such as incense wafting oddly, a single candle's flame flickering, etc.

Now that the King has arrived, ask him to summon the minor daemon you have in your petition, and then read the petition out loud. Really mean it when you speak.

Then pause a moment, and try to hear the reply from the other spirit.

If you are having trouble, re-read the chapter on hearing spirits. Just know that after the summoning, the King will be there and quite aware of your petition.

Spend a minute or more on visualizing the manifestation of your desire. Go into detail.

Now, time for the ritual specific candle. As you light this candle, ask the King:

King Asmodeus! I ask that you bless this candle to bring about my desire!

After lighting the ritual candle, you can either burn the petition and drop it into the fireproof bowl, or keep the petition in a safe place away from prying eyes.

Pause another moment and now give thanks to the King for attending to your petition and give the sacrifice.

Prick a finger (any finger, doesn't matter) and place a drop or two of your blood onto the smaller sigil. Touch the sigil to a candle flame (ANY candle on the altar), and while it burns in the fireproof bowl, say:

King Asmodeus! (*Summoned minor daemon, ex: Nitika!*)! I now humbly offer to you a drop of my essence, in return for you acting upon this request!

After the paper has burned away, stir the ashes to make sure it's completely burned away. The ashes should be tossed outside after the ritual.

To close the ritual, you can ask the King to depart as follows:

King Asmodeus! I now give you leave to depart, departing in peace and to come again when I next call.

That is it.

Allow the small, ritual candle to burn out completely. If you can't burn it safely on the altar, carefully move it to a safe area. I usually use a bathtub or empty fireplace. You could use the center of your stove top or even put the candle in a cold oven, on a cookie sheet, which prevents wax from spilling onto the oven bottom.

Now, the hardest part; Walk away from the altar and put the issue out of your mind. Trust in the King to deliver, and put doubt out of your mind.

Pathworking King Asmodeus & Minor Daemon

For this, you will need your petition, the smaller Asmodeus Master Sigil for the sacrifice, plus lancet and fireproof bowl and a lighter.

Settle yourself in and get relaxed. If possible, go into an Alpha state. Before beginning, just after you've relaxed, protect yourself. The very best way is to surround yourself with golden light. You do this by imagining a golden light starting in your heart center, which spreads out to surround your entire body, out to a few feet. Allow this gold light to solidify, which creates impenetrable energy barrier to any non-beneficial energies you might encounter.

Visualize each of the following images. Try to see as much detail as possible.

> **You are at the base of a tall mountain at night**
> **At the top is a massive castle**
> **You now are in a long hallway, and you walk to a red door at the end**
> **Open the door. It's a huge office.**
> **You now see a raised dais. King Asmodeus is seated on a grand throne.**

(His appearance may shift, but expect a big man, gray skin, wearing a silver crown).

Without hesitation, read your petition. Then tell him what you offer for his help, and that you need (Daemon's name or just say "a minor daemon") to help with this.

Asmodeus may clap, or he may simply wave, and a door opens near the dais.

Out will walk a minor demon. Pay close attention to this one's appearance. You may, or may not, hear the daemon's name.

Greet the minor daemon. Read your petition again, addressing this daemon.

Take a moment to fully visual the outcome of your petition, how it feels. Make this as real as possible.

The minor daemon may or may not react. But all you need to do at this point is make your request.

At this point, turn to the King and make a gesture of thanks and farewell.

The King will clap his hands -

And you find yourself where you were before starting this pathworking.

Now, make sure to work the sacrifice. Again, this needs to be a small drop of blood onto the small combined sigil. Burn this, allowing it to burn in the bowl. Make sure it is totally consumed.

CHAPTER FOUR

King of the Jinn

The original concept behind the term "Jinn" means "helper spirit" or "daemon".

My experience has been that the Jinn are more like the "Fire Elementals" one is likely to encounter in Islamic lore and myths. So, in addition to the idea that Asmodeus can assist you in controlling the "Genius" spirits, he can also give you assistance when we wish to work with the Jinn.

As I have previously cautioned, there is no pathworking for this type of Asmodeus magick. He is their king, so he can command them to appear without all the extra fuss of calling on archangels and other guardian spirits. Asmodeus can not only control a Jinn, in the same manner older rituals use archangels to control the more unruly daemons, but he will quickly locate a Jinn who can assist you in manifesting a desire.

Ask nicely, and give a good reason, such as the attention of a potential partner, and ask the King for a Romance or Family Jinn, and the King will bring to you the Jinn most suited what you desire, and then keep an eye on the Jinn while the desire begins to manifest. The Jinn can be literalists, meaning that if your petition is in ANY WAY vague, it gives the Jinn too much room to not deliver your desire, and might make your situation worse.

Although Asmodeus can control the Jinn, but he will also step back and allow the Jinn to work. Even if that means the Jinn will deliver chaos instead of your desire, if Asmodeus feels you might learn something from the chaos. But Asmodeus will also decline to assist you if he feels that what you are asking is either not in your best interest, or is impractical to deliver.

Your Petition

A brief word about the petition for this ritual. You should spell out the TYPE of Jinn you are needing, and what you wish to manifest. The following example is just that, an example.

"King Asmodeus, I humbly ask that you locate and bring to me a _____ JINN, and that this JINN work tirelessly until my request manifests. I ask that this JINN bring to me_____"

Or words to that effect.

Types of Jinn

Older writings on the Jinn have helped define who the Jinn are, and their shapes and myths have evolved over time. In popular culture, mostly in the western world, the Jinn is associated with the Persian-looking beings who'll spring from an old lamp, leaving a trail of vapor. This "Genie" will then deliver a few wishes in return for this freedom. This type of Jinn often has a sense of humor and is played for laughs.

We'll not be working with the popular concept of the Jinn. We'll be working with the legendary, hard to control, elusive fire angelic beings. These guys don't get played for laughs.

Asmodeus indicates that there are multiple types of Jinn. There's the traditional Fire Jinn, most often summoned during a typical Jinn ritual.

Aside from the usual Fire Jinn, we have Wealth Jinn, Family Jinn, Progress Jinn, Inspiration Jinn, Chaos Jinn (and his counter-part), the Order Jinn, a Jinn to help find lost objects (maybe I can finally locate my sanity), and the ever-popular Love Jinn.

During my practice runs while defining these rituals, I worked a ritual where I tasked Asmodeus to bring into the circle a Jinn who can give me advice for this chapter. Asmodeus brought a group of smaller beings, several tiny points of reddish light, who communicated to me I was to call them "Ak-Ta-Lak-Ah", and they would assist me. I wanted to know as much about them as possible.

A very diverse, and somewhat underutilized, group of magickal spirits, the Jinn can be quite a handful if approached incorrectly. As with the other deities and daemons I've written about, do not supplicate yourself to a Jinn, because then they'll eagerly accept the energy of your sacrifice, only to deliver nothing in return.

King Asmodeus is a bit more cooperative than summoning a Jinn alone, and he will simply bring to you a Jinn-spirit which matches your desire, and then he compels them to work for you. This by-passes a lot of extra ritualistic steps, some of which involve entrapping the Jinn into objects or crystals. King Asmodeus is more like "You heard the petition, and you must do as asked, or suffer." Or words to that effect.

My tests, which included getting a money Jinn to maintain income while writing non-magick projects, is working and working very well.

Let's take a look at a Master Ritual, which can be modified for most any purpose.

King of the Jinn Master Ritual

This is a ritual designed for you to modify to fit your own needs.

This ritual can be as complex as you wish to make it, or be a simple ritual with a single candle (red preferred), Jinn Master sigil, and your petition.

Since the Jinn are basically fire elementals, use colors that represent fire, such as orange or red. Multiple candles are recommended, and I will use six total when working this ritual. In the more elaborate ritual, I recommend using items to represent all elements, Earth, Fire, Water, and Air. This means candles, goblet with water, crystals, and incense.

Decide on which Jinn type you will need, as this factors into your initial approach and petition.

For a full ritual, here's what you'll need:
Multiple altar candles (orange or red)
King Asmodeus' Jinn Sigil
Candle specific for Jinn Magick (Gold or Red)
A small version of the sigil for the sacrifice
A small glass of water
Crystals (Earth)
Incense (any stick or resin)
Fire proof bowl

Diabetic lancet

Your prepared petition

Once you have your altar set up, in any manner you choose, you can begin the ritual. Begin with casting a circle for protection. The Jinn are tricky enough all on their own, but combined with Asmodeus, you really need a standard circle to be fully protected.

Define your circle, and then stand in the center. Stand with your right arm lifted, pointing in each direction as you summon the guardians. After saying each phrase, draw a simple pentacle in the air with a finger or wand:

Turn so that you are facing east and say:

"I now call upon the guardian of the east - Lucifer! Renich Tasa Uberaca Biasa Icar, Lucifer!"

Turn to the south and say:

"I now call upon the guardian of the south, Flereous! Ganic Tasa fubin, Flereous!"

Turn to the west and say:

"I now call upon the guardian of the west, Leviathan! Jedan Tasa hoet naca, Leviathan!"

Turn to the north and say:

"I now call upon the guardian of the north, Belial! Lirach tasa vefa welhc Belial!"

Finally, hold your arms up, and say to the sky: **"I now**

summon Satan, Ave Satanis! Satan, keep guard over this sacred space! This circle is sealed, and all unwanted and uninvited energies must depart my space now!"

I'll often wing it here, and say something like "Bugger off!"

Main summoning:

Sit or stand facing your altar. Gaze upon the sigil. Then, summon King Asmodeus by saying his King of the Jinn ENN three times:

Malik Al-jini Malik Allahab 'ana 'astadeik
Malik Al-jini Malik Allahab 'ana 'astadeik
Malik Al-jini Malik Allahab 'ana 'astadeik
King Asmodeus, I now summon you!
Join with me! Be with me in my space!

Pause a few moments. At this point, look to see any signs the King is nearby, such as incense wafting oddly, a single candle's flame flickering, etc.

Now that the King has arrived, you need the specific Jinn to be called.

King of the Jinn, I now ask that you compel a (type of) Jinn to do my bidding, namely, (list your needs and desire)

After speaking, be quiet for a moment or two, and see what the reply might be. The arrival of the Jinn might be detected by watching the candles. One or more of the candles might begin to sputter, the flame grows, as the Jinn appears. Stay quiet for a few moments.

If you are having trouble, re-read the section on hearing spirits. Just know that after the summoning, the Jinn will be there and quite aware of your petition.

Read the petition aloud. Really mean it when you speak.

Spend a minute or more on visualizing the manifestation of your desire. Go into detail.

Now, time for the ritual specific candle. As you light this candle, ask the King:

King Asmodeus! I ask that you bless this candle to bring about my desire!

After lighting the ritual candle, you can either burn the petition and drop it into the fireproof bowl, or keep the petition in a safe place away from prying eyes.

Pause another moment and now give thanks to the King for attending to your petition and give the sacrifice.

Prick a finger (any finger, doesn't matter) and place a drop or two of your blood onto the smaller sigil. Touch the sigil to a candle flame (ANY candle on the altar), and while it burns in the fireproof bowl, say:

King Asmodeus! I now humbly offer to you a drop of my essence, in return for you acting upon this request!

After the paper has burned away, stir the ashes to make

sure it's completely burned away. The ashes should be tossed outside after the ritual.

To close the ritual, you can ask the King to depart as follows:

King Asmodeus! This ritual is now complete. Have the JINN stay and work magick for me, and I now give you leave to depart, departing in peace and to come again when I next call. The JINN may only depart once the magick has manifested!

That is it.

Allow the small, ritual candle to burn out completely. If you can't burn it safely on the altar, carefully move it to a safe area. I usually use a bathtub or empty fireplace. You could use the center of your stove top or even put the candle in a cold oven, on a cookie sheet, which prevents wax from spilling onto the oven bottom.

Now, the hardest part; Walk away from the altar and put the issue out of your mind. Trust in the King to deliver, and put doubt out of your mind.

Releasing the Jinn.

Sometimes they stay on even after they're finished and the magick has manifested. In that case, they might become a nuisance. So, once your desire has manifested, make sure to go back into ritual. You will also need a second offering/sacrifice for both King Asmodeus and the Jinn who stayed behind.

Use a small version of the King's JINN sigil, and drop some blood onto it.

Light the altar candles

Summon King Asmodeus:

> **Malik Al-jini Malik Allahab 'ana 'astadeik**
> **Malik Al-jini Malik Allahab 'ana 'astadeik**
> **Malik Al-jini Malik Allahab 'ana 'astadeik**
> **King Asmodeus, I now summon you!**
> **Join with me! Be with me in my space!**

Give him a moment to arrive. Then say:

> **King Asmodeus! My desire has manifested!**
> **I now ask that you release the Jinn working for me.**
> **And by way of thanks, I now humbly offer a drop of my essence in gratitude for the work you did on my behalf.**

Touch the sigil to a candle flame, and allow it to fully burn in the fire-proof bowl.

Money-Specific JINN Ritual

Like the generic JINN ritual, you will need the King Asmodeus JINN sigil, and perhaps some "Joss" paper, or Hell-Money bank notes, with the JINN sigil drawn on them in ink.

Use green ink, if possible, for your petition, or a fine line marker in gold. I use a "Sharpie" gold fine line marker for a lot of my money petitions. Write your petition with this ink, and then sign it using the magick ink talked about in the preparations segment of Chapter 2. You can also use this ink on the Joss paper.

The petition can be worded as follows: *"**King Asmodeus, King of the Jinn! I ask that you bring to me a wealth Jinn, one who can work quickly, for I desire that my bank account swell with money, tens of thousands of (US or your currency) dollars! I ask that this Jinn bring this to me in a safe manner, harming none.**"*

For a full ritual, here's what you'll need:

Multiple altar candles (gold and green, silver and green)
King Asmodeus' Jinn Sigil
Gold candle, anointed with oil.
A small version of the sigil for the sacrifice
A small glass of water
Crystals (Earth)

Incense (any stick or resin)

Fire proof bowl

Diabetic lancet

Your prepared petition

Once you have your altar set up, in any manner you choose, you can begin the ritual. Begin with casting a circle for protection. The Jinn are tricky enough all on their own, but combined with Asmodeus, you really need a standard circle to be fully protected.

Define your circle, and then stand in the center. Stand with your right arm lifted, pointing in each direction as you summon the guardians. After saying each phrase, draw a simple pentacle in the air with a finger or wand:

Turn so that you are facing east and say:

"I now call upon the guardian of the east - Lucifer! Renich Tasa Uberaca Biasa Icar, Lucifer!"

Turn to the south and say:

"I now call upon the guardian of the south, Flereous! Ganic Tasa fubin, Flereous!"

Turn to the west and say:

"I now call upon the guardian of the west, Leviathan! Jedan Tasa hoet naca, Leviathan!"

Turn to the north and say:

"I now call upon the guardian of the north, Belial!

Lirach tasa vefa welhc Belial!"

Finally, hold your arms up, and say to the sky: **"I now summon Satan, Ave Satanis! Satan, keep guard over this sacred space! This circle is sealed, and all unwanted and uninvited energies must depart my space now!"**

Main summoning:

Sit or stand facing your altar. Gaze upon the sigil. Then, summon King Asmodeus by saying his King of the Jinn ENN three times:

> **Malik Al-jini Malik Allahab 'ana 'astadeik**
> **Malik Al-jini Malik Allahab 'ana 'astadeik**
> **Malik Al-jini Malik Allahab 'ana 'astadeik**
> **King Asmodeus, I now summon you!**
> **Join with me! Be with me in my space!**

Pause a few moments. At this point, look to see any signs the King is nearby, such as incense wafting oddly, a single candle's flame flickering, etc.

Now that the King has arrived, you need the specific Jinn to be called.

> **King of the Jinn, I now ask that you compel a wealth Jinn to do my bidding, namely, fill my bank account with money, thousands of dollars, and that it comes to me in a safe manner, harming none.**

After speaking, be quiet for a moment or two, and see what the reply might be. The arrival of the Jinn might be detected by watching the candles. One or more of the candles might begin to sputter, the flame grows, as the Jinn appears. Stay quiet for a few moments.

If you are having trouble, re-read the section on hearing spirits. Just know that after the summoning, the Jinn will be there and quite aware of your petition.

Read the petition aloud. Really mean it when you speak.

Spend a minute or more on visualizing the manifestation of your desire. Go into detail.

Now, time for the gold candle. As you light this candle, ask the King:

King of the Jinn, Asmodeus, I ask that you bless this magick candle to bring about (what you want)!

After lighting the ritual candle, you can either burn the petition and drop it into the fireproof bowl, or keep the petition in a safe place away from prying eyes.

Pause another moment and now give thanks to the King for attending to your petition and give the sacrifice.

Prick a finger (any finger, doesn't matter) and place a drop or two of your blood onto the smaller sigil. Touch the sigil to a candle flame (ANY candle on the altar), and while it burns in the fireproof bowl, say:

King Asmodeus! I now humbly offer to you a drop

of my essence, in return for you acting upon this request!

After the paper has burned away, stir the ashes to make sure it's completely burned away. The ashes should be tossed outside after the ritual.

You can also burn the "Hell Money" at this point, even combining it with the offering by placing a single drop of blood onto it, with the sigil design.

To close the ritual, you can ask the King to depart as follows:

King Asmodeus! This ritual is now complete. Have the JINN stay and work magick for me, and I now give you leave to depart, departing in peace and to come again when I next call. The JINN may only depart once the magick has manifested!

That is it.

Allow the small, ritual candle to burn out completely. If you can't burn it safely on the altar, carefully move it to a safe area. I usually use a bathtub or empty fireplace. You could use the center of your stove top or even put the candle in a cold oven, on a cookie sheet, which prevents wax from spilling onto the oven bottom.

Now, the hardest part; Walk away from the altar and put the issue out of your mind. Trust in the King to deliver, and put doubt out of your mind.

Releasing the Jinn.

Sometimes they stay on well past when the magick has manifested, and some might become a nuisance. So, once your desire has manifested, make sure to go back into ritual. You will also need a second offering/sacrifice for both King Asmodeus and the Jinn who stayed behind.

This can be your blood on the small sigil, or on a piece of "Hell Money" with the sigil drawn on it.

Light the altar candles

Summon King Asmodeus:

> **Malik Al-jini Malik Allahab 'ana 'astadeik**
> **Malik Al-jini Malik Allahab 'ana 'astadeik**
> **Malik Al-jini Malik Allahab 'ana 'astadeik**
> **King Asmodeus, I now summon you!**
> **Join with me! Be with me in my space!**

Give him a moment to arrive. Then say:

> **King Asmodeus! My desire has manifested!**
> **I now ask that you release the Jinn working for me,**
> **And by way of thanks, I now humbly offer a drop of my essence in gratitude for the work you did on my behalf.**

Touch the sigil to a candle flame, and allow it to fully burn in the fire-proof bowl.

Love (Lust) JINN Ritual

Like the generic JINN ritual, you will need the King Asmodeus JINN sigil. If you have a specific person in mind, you need their photo.

Decide if this is to be a LUST ritual, or LOVE ritual. Items specific to **LUST are in bold**, *LOVE in Bold Italics*. Colors are: Red for lust. Pink for love.

While preparing your petition, also print out a photo on a color printer. Make some RED magick ink, and using this ink, write on the back their name, then YOUR name, then circle your names three times.

Use this special ink for the petition as well.

The petition can be worded as follows: *"**King Asmodeus, King of the Jinn! I ask that you bring to me a LOVE/LUST Jinn, one who can work quickly, for I desire that my heart's desire, this person (holdup photo), be brought to me, that He/Her heart is open to being with me.**"*

For a full ritual, here's what you'll need:
   Multiple altar candles (white, black, red, pink)
   King Asmodeus' Jinn Sigil
   Red/*Pink* candle, anointed with oil.
   A small version of the sigil for the sacrifice
   A small glass of water

Crystals (Earth)

Incense (any stick or resin)

Fire proof bowl

Diabetic lancet

Your prepared petition

Once you have your altar set up, in any manner you choose, you can begin the ritual. Begin with casting a circle for protection. The Jinn are tricky enough all on their own, but combined with Asmodeus, you really need a standard circle to be fully protected.

Define your circle, and then stand in the center. Stand with your right arm lifted, pointing in each direction as you summon the guardians. After saying each phrase, draw a simple pentacle in the air with a finger or wand:

Turn so that you are facing east and say:

"I now call upon the guardian of the east - Lucifer! Renich Tasa Uberaca Biasa Icar, Lucifer!"

Turn to the south and say:

"I now call upon the guardian of the south, Flereous! Ganic Tasa fubin, Flereous!"

Turn to the west and say:

"I now call upon the guardian of the west, Leviathan! Jedan Tasa hoet naca, Leviathan!"

Turn to the north and say:

"I now call upon the guardian of the north, Belial! Lirach tasa vefa welhc Belial!"

Finally, hold your arms up, and say to the sky: **"I now summon Satan, Ave Satanis! Satan, keep guard over this sacred space! This circle is sealed, and all unwanted and uninvited energies must depart my space now!"**

Main summoning:

Sit or stand facing your altar. Gaze upon the sigil. Then, summon King Asmodeus by saying his King of the Jinn ENN three times:

> **Malik Al-jini Malik Allahab 'ana 'astadeik**
> **Malik Al-jini Malik Allahab 'ana 'astadeik**
> **Malik Al-jini Malik Allahab 'ana 'astadeik**
> **King Asmodeus, I now summon you!**
> **Join with me! Be with me in my space!**

Pause a few moments. At this point, look to see any signs the King is nearby, such as incense wafting oddly, a single candle's flame flickering, etc.

Now that the King has arrived, you need the specific Jinn to be called.

King of the Jinn, I now ask that you compel a (LUST/*LOVE*) Jinn to do my bidding, namely, bring to me my heart's desire!"

After speaking, be quiet for a moment or two, and see what the reply might be. The arrival of the Jinn might be detected by watching the candles. One or more of the candles might begin to sputter, the flame grows, as the Jinn appears. Stay quiet for a few moments.

If you are having trouble, re-read the section on hearing spirits. Just know that after the summoning, the Jinn will be there and quite aware of your petition.

Read the petition aloud. Really mean it when you speak.

Spend a minute or more on visualizing the manifestation of your desire. Go into detail.

Now, time for the ritual specific candle. As you light this candle, ask the King:

King of the Jinn, Asmodeus, I ask that you bless this candle to bring about my desire!

After lighting the ritual candle, you can either burn the petition and drop it into the fireproof bowl, or keep the petition in a safe place away from prying eyes.

Pause another moment and now give thanks to the King for attending to your petition and give the sacrifice.

Prick a finger (any finger, doesn't matter) and place a drop or two of your blood onto the smaller sigil. Touch the sigil to a candle flame (ANY candle on the altar), and while it burns in the fireproof bowl, say:

King Asmodeus! I now humbly offer to you a drop

of my essence, in return for you acting upon this request!

After the paper has burned away, stir the ashes to make sure it's completely burned away. The ashes should be tossed outside after the ritual.

To close the ritual, you can ask the King to depart as follows:

King Asmodeus! This ritual is now complete. Have the JINN stay and work magick for me, and I now give you leave to depart, departing in peace and to come again when I next call. The JINN may only depart once the magick has manifested!

That is it.

Allow the small, ritual candle to burn out completely. If you can't burn it safely on the altar, carefully move it to a safe area. I usually use a bathtub or empty fireplace. You could use the center of your stove top or even put the candle in a cold oven, on a cookie sheet, which prevents wax from spilling onto the oven bottom.

Now, the hardest part; Walk away from the altar and put the issue out of your mind. Trust in the King to deliver, and put doubt out of your mind.

Releasing the Jinn.

Sometimes they stay on well past when the magick has manifested, and some might become a nuisance. So, once your desire has manifested, make sure to go back into ritual. You will also need a second offering/sacrifice for both King Asmodeus and the Jinn who stayed behind.

For the sacrifice, stick with the time-honored drop of blood on the King's sigil.

    Light the altar candles
    Summon King Asmodeus:
        Malik Al-jini Malik Allahab 'ana 'astadeik
        Malik Al-jini Malik Allahab 'ana 'astadeik
        Malik Al-jini Malik Allahab 'ana 'astadeik
        King Asmodeus, I now summon you!
        Join with me! Be with me in my space!
    Give him a moment to arrive. Then say:
        King Asmodeus! My desire has manifested!
        I now ask that you release the Jinn working for me,
        And by way of thanks, I now humbly offer a drop of my essence in gratitude for the work you did on my behalf.

    Touch the sigil to a candle flame, and allow it to fully burn in the fire-proof bowl.

CHAPTER FIVE

Hell's Banker

Honestly, I dislike most bankers. I've always felt as if they were simply looking for ways to "fee" me to death, bleeding my accounts dry with "maintenance" fees, deposit fees, etc. (I'm not kidding. Several banks charge deposit fees when you have a business checking account. I'm talking the big banks, not just those low-end, gonna-rip-you-off, banks found in big box retail super stores.)

Asmodeus is really no different. He will look for ways to trip you up and not assist you in manifesting wealth and riches. So, let's tread carefully while working with this aspect.

One unique thing you might want to try is using "Hell Money", or "Joss Paper" in a ritual to Asmodeus, the Banker. The idea behind this is to burn it, converting it into astral money, and then deceased relative or specific deities will have some spending cash. You could also pick up some of the very thin gold foil to burn, and this is often found with the Hell Money, or a simple search online. In this case, Google is your friend. Many Asian or Indian grocery stores will stock these as well.

I figure, when dealing with money matters, it doesn't hurt to try this. A few years ago, I went through several packets of these things just testing them. They burn very quickly, and make for some interesting patterns as the fiber burns. My notes indicate these Hell Money notes do work, but don't expect anything long lasting.

You can combine a Hell Money note with the Banker's sigil drawn onto it, plus a drop of blood. Sending over a few million "Hell Dollars" to Asmodeus might set you apart from the other magicians summoning Asmodeus on a weekly basis.

One would think green would be the candle colors here, but Asmodeus communicated to me that money is of many differing colors, and that gold or silver are unambiguous in their meaning. But you can use green if you do not have any gold candles. Buying the smaller spell or chime candles work in these rituals. I prefer those to other candles because they burn quickly and I'm not worrying all day if a glass-encased candle is going to break the glass and cause a problem.

With all the other items on the altar, make gold the primary color for this. I have a huge altar cloth that is decorated in gold, which I use for any rituals involving money or income.

The master ritual to Asmodeus as the banker is almost the same as the King of Daemons ritual, except we're working only with Asmodeus, and not asking him to supervise a lower daemon.

We will use Asmodeus' classic ENN, as it works best no matter what aspect you call upon.

The Draw Riches Ritual

Items Needed:

    Altar Candles

    Gold candles, or silver (green in a pinch)

    Incense - frankincense or any other traditional incense

    King Asmodeus' Banker sigil

    Crystals to represent Earth. Or some special (to you) rocks.

    A goblet or wine glass of water

    Small copy of the sigil for the sacrifice, or a Hell Dollar

    Diabetic lancet

    Fire-resistant bowl

Prepare your space

Arrange your altar in any way that suits you. Get the incense going. If using a charcoal puck, light it and allow it to become covered in ash.

Light all the candles (except for the gold candle). Room

lights out.

Prepare the ritual-specific candle for use in ritual. I typically will place a drop of mineral oil onto the candle and coat it lightly. Then I secure it into a solid holder, as this candle should be burned completely after the ritual. Keep it in a safe place if you use a temporary altar.

Circle Casting

If you have the space, draw a circle on the floor with chalk. This will help define the perimeter of the sacred space. If not, don't worry. As long as you can define the circle using a crystal point, athame/dagger, or even your finger.

Make sure you have everything will need in your space.

Define your circle, and then stand in the center. Stand with your right arm lifted, pointing in each direction as you summon the guardians. After saying each phrase, draw a simple pentacle in the air with a finger or wand:

Turn so that you are facing east and say:

"I now call upon the guardian of the east - Lucifer! Renich Tasa Uberaca Biasa Icar, Lucifer!"

Turn to the south and say:

"I now call upon the guardian of the south, Flereous! Ganic Tasa fubin, Flereous!"

Turn to the west and say:

"I now call upon the guardian of the west, Leviathan!

Jedan Tasa hoet naca, Leviathan!"

Turn to the north and say:

"I now call upon the guardian of the north, Belial! Lirach tasa vefa welhc Belial!"

Finally, hold your arms up, and say to the sky: **"I now summon Satan, Ave Satanis! Satan, keep guard over this sacred space! This circle is sealed, and all unwanted and uninvited energies must depart my space now!"**

Main summoning:

Sit or stand facing your altar. Gaze upon the sigil. Then, summon King Asmodeus by saying his traditional ENN three times:

> **Ayer avage aloren Asmodeus aken**
> **Ayer avage aloren Asmodeus aken**
> **Ayer avage aloren Asmodeus aken**
> **King Asmodeus, I now summon you!**
> **Join with me! Be with me in my space!**

Pause a few moments. At this point, look to see any signs the King is nearby, such as incense wafting oddly, a single candle's flame flickering, etc.

Now that the King has arrived, you speak to him about your petition. After speaking, be quiet for a moment or two, and see what the reply might be.

If you are having trouble, re-read the section on hearing

spirits. Just know that after the summoning, the King will be there and quite aware of your petition.

Read the petition aloud. Really mean it when you speak.

Spend a minute or more on visualizing the manifestation of your desire. Go into detail.

Now, time for the ritual specific candle. As you light this candle, ask the King:

King Asmodeus! I ask that you bless this candle to bring about my desire!

After lighting the ritual candle, you can either burn the petition and drop it into the fireproof bowl, or keep the petition in a safe place away from prying eyes.

Pause another moment and now give thanks to the King for attending to your petition and give the sacrifice.

Prick a finger (any finger, doesn't matter) and place a drop or two of your blood onto the smaller sigil. Touch the sigil to a candle flame (ANY candle on the altar), and while it burns in the fireproof bowl, say:

King Asmodeus! I now humbly offer to you a drop of my essence, in return for you acting upon this request!

After the paper has burned away, stir the ashes to make sure it's completely burned away. The ashes should be tossed outside after the ritual.

To close the ritual, you can ask the King to depart as follows:

King Asmodeus! I now give you leave to depart, departing in peace and to come again when I next call.

That is it.

Allow the small, ritual candle to burn out completely. If you can't burn it safely on the altar, carefully move it to a safe area. I usually use a bathtub or empty fireplace. You could use the center of your stove top or even put the candle in a cold oven, on a cookie sheet, which prevents wax from spilling onto the oven bottom.

Now, the hardest part; Walk away from the altar and put the issue out of your mind. Trust in the King to deliver, and put doubt out of your mind.

Pathworking Asmodeus as the Banker

For this, you will need your petition, the smaller Asmodeus Master Sigil for the sacrifice, plus lancet and fireproof bowl and a lighter.

Settle yourself in and get relaxed. If possible, go into an Alpha state. Before beginning, just after you've relaxed, protect yourself. The very best way is to surround yourself with golden light. You do this by imagining a golden light starting in your heart center, which spreads out to surround your entire body, out to a few feet. Allow this gold light to solidify, which creates impenetrable energy barrier to any non-beneficial energies you might encounter.

Visualize each of the following images. Try to see as much detail as possible.

You are standing outside a large building, looking up at it, taller than the clouds.

You are now inside a massive and ornate bank lobby

A small minor daemon will greet you. Tell it you are there to see The Banker.

It will wave you to a small elevator.

Step inside, and you are whisked upwards.

Step out of the elevator, and there's Asmodeus behind a huge desk.

Walk boldly to him, and hand him your petition, and explain why you need it manifested into your life.

Take a moment to fully visualize the new money coming into your life.

He might nod, or he may just write on the petition. Leave the petition, and thank Asmodeus for helping you.

To exit, you turn, and go the elevator.

As the door opens, you find yourself back where you began, in your own space.

Now, make sure to work the sacrifice. Again, this needs to be a small drop of blood onto the King's small sigil. Burn this, allowing it to burn in the bowl. Make sure it is totally consumed by the fire.

CHAPTER SIX

Asmodeus - Demon of Wrath

Note the spelling, "demon". We'll be working with a real nasty aspect of Asmodeus. Make doubly sure your target deserves this treatment.

Asmodeus is well known in many circles as the ultimate revenge demon. A friend asked for a nasty revenge thing for a guy who gaslighted her and tried to break up her marriage. Once I talked to her, I felt the need was there for a nice, horrid revenge ritual.

So, I did a more traditional ritual to the King.

In a week, I was sent a screen grab of a post by the target, lamenting about how they'd been fired as they'd failed a drug test. A week later, the target is running a go-fund-me to help with rent. It might have raised a tiny percentage of what they needed. Last we'd heard, this person was evicted and seemed to have disappeared with their drug habit taking hold of them. I can only hope they eventually rehabilitated and turned it around.

Again, I have to make this clear: Make absolutely sure your target deserves the treatment that Asmodeus in this aspect will deliver.

And he *will* deliver.

Another example:

A few years ago, a client came to me and asked for retribution for a man who'd not only drained her bank account, but had committed fraud ALL while pretending to be a boyfriend. She'd gotten tired of waiting for the police to do anything, and she sought me out.

I immediately heard "Asmodeus". So I used the traditional ENN and sigil to ask Asmodeus to drop by, and give me ideas. He arrived in my temple space, and it was suggested I just explain the crimes committed, and he'd deliver just punishment in the name of my client. I then wrote up the petition and gave him a drop of my blood.

The report from my client was interesting: The target got into a car wreck, and while dealing with the cops on scene, he was arrested for DUI, as well as having a few traffic tickets outstanding. He had quite a bad weekend.

Asmodeus in this aspect works quickly, and he'll dish out nasty events to anyone who asks him properly. Even if they don't deserve it, because if you ask him to bring bad luck or experiences to someone who doesn't deserve the treatment, he's going to deliver that to YOU, and not the target. I haven't tested this, but it was made clear to me during my first contact with King Asmodeus.

It's also very important to perform the full ritual, including the circle casting and ejection of unwanted energies/spirits/etc. Make sure to use the correct incense, as frankincense assists in clearing out unwanted energies.

Preparations

Preparing for this type of ritual involves getting some item that can be tied to the target. I have had clients send me clothing, small pieces of paper with their writing, and in one case, a small vial of saliva. All this ties the magick to the target.

This can also work with a photo and their name written on the back. Use red ink, or magick red ink.

Once you have the items to tie the magick to the target, you can write the petition. As with the other examples, this is just to give you an idea of how I word a petition.

"King Asmodeus! This person, (name) has (list of crimes or offenses). (Name) needs to be dealt with in the harshest ways. I leave this up to you, but make (name) suffer ten times what (name) has caused others to suffer."

Now, you're ready to get down to some serious cursing.

Wrath of Asmodeus Ritual

The basic colors to any cursing ritual should be all black. Black candles, black altar cloth, including a small chime candle in black.

You will prepare this candle with some black salt. To make black salt, crush a small piece of charcoal (incense charcoal, a bit of charred wood from a fireplace - see appendix). Coat the candle in some light oil, and roll it in the black salt.

Items Needed:

Altar Candles, reds and blacks.

Black candle prepared with black salt

Photo or some item connected to the target

Incense - frankincense. Needed to purify your space

King Asmodeus' Wrathful sigil

Crystals to represent Earth. Or some special (to you) rocks

A goblet or wine glass of water

Small copy of the sigil for the sacrifice

Diabetic lancet

Fire-resistant bowl

Prepare your space

Arrange your altar in any way that suits you. Get the

incense going. If using a charcoal puck, light it and allow it to become covered in ash.

Light all the candles (except for the candle for your desire). Room lights out.

Prepare the ritual-specific candle for use then secure it into a solid holder, as this candle should be burned completely after the ritual. Keep it in a safe place if you use a temporary altar.

Circle Casting

If you have the space, draw a circle on the floor with chalk. This will help define the perimeter of the sacred space. If not, don't worry. As long as you can define the circle using a crystal point, athame/dagger, or even your finger.

Make sure you have everything will need in your space.

Define your circle, and then stand in the center. Stand with your right arm lifted, pointing in each direction as you summon the guardians. After saying each phrase, draw a simple pentacle in the air with a finger or wand:

Turn so that you are facing east and say:

"I now call upon the guardian of the east - Lucifer! Renich Tasa Uberaca Biasa Icar, Lucifer!"

Turn to the south and say:

"I now call upon the guardian of the south, Flereous! Ganic Tasa fubin, Flereous!"

Turn the the west and say:

"I now call upon the guardian of the west, Leviathan! Jedan Tasa hoet naca, Leviathan!"

Turn to the north and say:

"I now call upon the guardian of the north, Belial! Lirach tasa vefa welhc Belial!"

Finally, hold your arms up, and say to the sky: *"I now summon Satan, Ave Satanis! Satan, keep guard over this sacred space! This circle is sealed, and all unwanted and uninvited energies must depart my space now!"*

Main summoning:

Sit or stand facing your altar. Gaze upon the sigil. Then, summon King Asmodeus by saying the aspect-specific ENN three times:

> *Imum Shargaz Ankah Eh Mum*
> *Imum Shargaz Ankah Eh Mum*
> *Imum Shargaz Ankah Eh Mum*
> *Wrathful King, Mighty King, hear me now!*
> *King Asmodeus the Wrathful, I now summon you!*
> *Join with me! Be with me in my space!*

Pause a few moments. At this point, look to see any signs the King is nearby, such as incense wafting oddly, a single candle's flame flickering, etc.

Now that the King has arrived, you speak to him about your petition. After speaking, be quiet for a moment or two, and see what the reply might be.

If you are having trouble, re-read the section on hearing spirits. Just know that after the summoning, the King will be there and quite aware of your petition.

Spend a minute or more on visualizing the manifestation of your desire. Go into detail.

Read your petition aloud. Really mean it when you speak.

Now, time for the ritual specific candle. As you light this candle, ask the King:

King Asmodeus! I ask that you bless this candle to curse this person (or bring down your wrath)!

After lighting the ritual candle, you can either burn the petition and drop it into the fireproof bowl, or keep the petition in a safe place away from prying eyes.

Pause another moment and now give thanks to the King for attending to your petition and give the sacrifice.

Prick a finger (any finger, doesn't matter) and place a drop or two of your blood onto the smaller sigil. Touch the sigil to a candle flame (ANY candle on the altar), and while it burns in the fireproof bowl, say:

King Asmodeus! I now humbly offer to you a drop of my essence, in return for you acting upon this request!

After the paper has burned away, stir the ashes to make sure it's completely burned away. The ashes should be tossed outside after the ritual.

To close the ritual, you can ask the King to depart as follows:

King Asmodeus! I now give you leave to depart, departing in peace and to come again when I next call.

That is it.

Allow the small, ritual candle to burn out completely. If you can't burn it safely on the altar, carefully move it to a safe area. I usually use a bathtub or empty fireplace. You could use the center of your stove top or even put the candle in a cold oven, on a cookie sheet, which prevents wax from spilling onto the oven bottom.

Now, the hardest part; Walk away from the altar and put the issue out of your mind. Trust in the King to deliver, and put doubt out of your mind.

Wrath of Asmodeus Ritual Pathworking

As with the standard ritual, please make sure your target really deserves this treatment.

You will need the smaller Wrath sigil along with your petition. You will also need a sterile lancet and a fire-safe bowl for the offering. It helps if you have a photo of the target for your wrath curse.

When ready, settle yourself in and allow yourself to relax into an alpha state, if you can. Before beginning, just after you've relaxed, protect yourself. The very best way is to surround yourself with golden light. You do this by imagining a golden light starting in your heart center, which spreads out to surround your entire body, out to a few feet. Allow this gold light to solidify, which creates impenetrable energy barrier to any non-beneficial energies you might encounter.

Visualize the following to the best of your ability.

You see a landscape of rugged mountains.

A flash of lightning.

Darkness, with swirling streamers of fog or smoke.

The smoke clears, revealing a large daemon in black.

He says "Are you sure?" and you need to answer him.

If your answer pleases this daemon, the fog will reappear and encircle you.

You now find yourself in a small library.

By the shelves is a large figure. Watch him as he turns towards you.

Present your petition. Go into detail, even if your written petition is short.

Pause and visualize your desire manifesting, the "karma" being visited on the target, and go into detail, and taking your time. Watch for his reaction, but know you were heard.

Say or project your gratitude for him listening to your petition.

Step back, and as you do, you are surrounded by fog.

At this point, you can wake up. As soon as you can, do the blood-offering using the Wrath sigil.

CHAPTER SEVEN

Master of Lust

I guess I can combine "love" in the romantic sense with the idea of "lust" and simply wanting to find a partner for the time being. The old "Love the one you're with" attitude.

Honestly, I've been "In Lust" far more often than I have been in love.

So, in this chapter, I will present two types of magick, one for just attracting a partner for a short time, and one for the ever-elusive "soul-mate".

I'm not about to begin a discussion about soul-mates. My only concern here is: Is the term two words, hyphenated words, or a single word? I'm going with hyphenated for this book.

Back when I was younger, I'd have used these rituals to draw women to me, as I know they work. But back then, in the dim, dark days of the early 1980s, I had no clue what I was doing when I did work with magick, so I just stumbled along.

Like with the Wrathful rituals, it's best to have some type of physical tie to the target of your heart's desire. Such as an article of clothing, a sample of their handwriting, but at the very least use a photograph and some red magick ink.

You could work either ritual to simply "draw" someone to you. Although I should suggest you also use a ritual from Chapter Three to make yourself more charismatic and attractive, THEN work one of these rituals. Work both, then attend an event or party, and see if anyone responds to your new energy.

The Draw Lust Ritual

Items Needed:

    Altar Candles

    Red chime candle for lust

    Item attached to the target or a photo

    Incense - frankincense or any other traditional incense

    King of Lust sigil

    Crystals to represent Earth. Or some special (to you) rocks.

    A goblet or wine glass of water

    Small copy of the sigil for the sacrifice

    Diabetic lancet

    Fire-resistant bowl

Prepare your space

Arrange your altar in any way that suits you. Get the incense going. If using a charcoal puck, light it and allow it to become covered in ash.

Light all the candles (except for the candle for your desire). Room lights out.

Prepare the ritual-specific candle for use in ritual. I typically will place a drop of mineral oil onto the candle and coat it lightly. Then I secure it into a solid holder, as this candle should be burned completely after the ritual. Keep it in a safe place if you use a temporary altar.

Circle Casting

If you have the space, draw a circle on the floor with chalk. This will help define the perimeter of the sacred space. If not, don't worry. As long as you can define the circle using a crystal point, athame/dagger, or even your finger.

Make sure you have everything will need in your space.

Define your circle, and then stand in the center. Stand with your right arm lifted, pointing in each direction as you summon the guardians. After saying each phrase, draw a simple pentacle in the air with a finger or wand:

Turn so that you are facing east and say:

"I now call upon the guardian of the east - Lucifer!

Renich Tasa Uberaca Biasa Icar, Lucifer!"

Turn to the south and say:

"I now call upon the guardian of the south, Flereous! Ganic Tasa fubin, Flereous!"

Turn to the west and say:

"I now call upon the guardian of the west, Leviathan! Jedan Tasa hoet naca, Leviathan!"

Turn to the north and say:

"I now call upon the guardian of the north, Belial! Lirach tasa vefa welhc Belial!"

Finally, hold your arms up, and say to the sky: **"I now summon Satan, Ave Satanis! Satan, keep guard over this sacred space! This circle is sealed, and all unwanted and uninvited energies must depart my space now!"**

Main summoning:

Sit or stand facing your altar. Gaze upon the sigil. Then, summon King Asmodeus by saying the aspect-specific ENN three times:

> **Lugal Ki Ta Lugal Hili**
> **Lugal Ki Ta Lugal Hili**
> **Lugal Ki Ta Lugal Hili**
> **King Asmodeus, I now summon you!**
> **King of Lust, join with me!**
> **Join with me! Be with me in my space!**

Pause a few moments. At this point, look to see any signs the King is nearby, such as incense wafting oddly, a single candle's flame flickering, etc.

Now that the King has arrived, you speak to him about your petition. After speaking, be quiet for a moment or two, and see what the reply might be.

If you are having trouble, re-read the section on hearing spirits. Just know that after the summoning, the King will be there and quite aware of your petition.

Read the petition aloud. Really mean it when you speak.

Spend a minute or more on visualizing the manifestation of your desire. Go into detail.

Now, time for the ritual specific candle. As you light this candle, ask the King:

King Asmodeus! I ask that you bless this candle to bring about my heart's desire!

After lighting the ritual candle, you can either burn the petition and drop it into the fireproof bowl, or keep the petition in a safe place away from prying eyes.

Pause another moment and now give thanks to the King for attending to your petition and give the sacrifice.

Prick a finger (any finger, doesn't matter) and place a drop or two of your blood onto the smaller sigil. Touch the sigil to a candle flame (ANY candle on the altar), and while it burns in the fireproof bowl, say:

King Asmodeus! I now humbly offer to you a drop of my essence, in return for you acting upon this request!

After the paper has burned away, stir the ashes to make sure it's completely burned away. The ashes should be tossed outside after the ritual.

To close the ritual, you can ask the King to depart as follows:

King Asmodeus! I now give you leave to depart, departing in peace and to come again when I next call.

That's it!

Allow the small, ritual candle to burn out completely. If you can't burn it safely on the altar, carefully move it to a safe area. I usually use a bathtub or empty fireplace. You could use the center of your stove top or even put the candle in a cold oven, on a cookie sheet, which prevents wax from spilling onto the oven bottom.

Now, the hardest part; Walk away from the altar and put the issue out of your mind. Trust in the King to deliver, and put doubt out of your mind.

The Draw Love Ritual

Like the Lust ritual, you will need a link to your target, and have it ready for this ritual.

Items Needed:

Altar Candles in Pinks, or go with white and black.

Small pink candle

Incense - frankincense or any other traditional incense

King Asmodeus' Love aspect master sigil

Crystals to represent Earth. Or some special (to you) rocks.

A goblet or wine glass of water

Target's item (or photo)

Small copy of the sigil for the sacrifice

Diabetic lancet

Fire-resistant bowl

Prepare your space

Arrange your altar in any way that suits you. Get the incense going. If using a charcoal puck, light it and allow it to become covered in ash.

Light all the candles (except for the candle for your desire). Room lights out.

Prepare the ritual-specific candle for use in ritual. I typically will place a drop of mineral oil onto the candle and coat it lightly. Then I secure it into a solid holder, as this candle should be burned completely after the ritual. Keep it in a safe place if you use a temporary altar.

Circle Casting

If you have the space, draw a circle on the floor with chalk. This will help define the perimeter of the sacred space. If not, don't worry. As long as you can define the circle using a crystal point, athame/dagger, or even your finger.

Make sure you have everything will need in your space.

Stand in the center of the circle. Stand with your right arm lifted, pointing in each direction as you summon the guardians. After saying each phrase, draw a simple pentacle in the air with a finger or wand:

Turn so that you are facing east and say:

"I now call upon the guardian of the east - Lucifer! Renich Tasa Uberaca Biasa Icar, Lucifer!"

Turn to the south and say:

"I now call upon the guardian of the south, Flereous! Ganic Tasa fubin, Flereous!"

Turn to the west and say:

"I now call upon the guardian of the west, Leviathan! Jedan Tasa hoet naca, Leviathan!"

Turn to the north and say:

"I now call upon the guardian of the north, Belial! Lirach tasa vefa welhc Belial!"

Finally, hold your arms up, and say to the sky: **"I now summon Satan, Ave Satanis! Satan, keep guard over this sacred space! This circle is sealed, and all unwanted and uninvited energies must depart my space now!"**

Main summoning:

Sit or stand facing your altar. Gaze upon the sigil. Then, summon King Asmodeus by saying the aspect-specific ENN three times:

> **Lugal Ki Ta Lugal Hili**
> **Lugal Ki Ta Lugal Hili**
> **Lugal Ki Ta Lugal Hili**
> **King Asmodeus, I now summon you!**
> **King of Love, join with me!**
> **Join with me! Be with me in my space!**

Pause a few moments. At this point, look to see any signs the King is nearby, such as incense wafting oddly, a single candle's flame flickering, etc.

Now that the King has arrived, you speak to him about your petition. After speaking, be quiet for a moment or two, and see what the reply might be.

If you are having trouble, re-read the section on hearing spirits. Just know that after the summoning, the King will be there and quite aware of your petition.

Read the petition aloud. Really mean it when you speak.

Spend a minute or more on visualizing the manifestation of your desire. Go into detail.

Now, time for the ritual specific candle. As you light this candle, ask the King:

King Asmodeus! I ask that you bless this candle to bring about my heart's desire!

After lighting the ritual candle, you can either burn the petition and drop it into the fireproof bowl, or keep the petition in a safe place away from prying eyes.

Pause another moment and now give thanks to the King for attending to your petition and give the sacrifice.

Prick a finger (any finger, doesn't matter) and place a drop or two of your blood onto the smaller sigil. Touch the sigil to a candle flame (ANY candle on the altar), and while it burns in the fireproof bowl, say:

King Asmodeus! I now humbly offer to you a drop of my essence, in return for you acting upon this request!

After the paper has burned away, stir the ashes to make sure it's completely burned away. The ashes should be tossed outside after the ritual.

To close the ritual, you can ask the King to depart as follows:

King Asmodeus! I now give you leave to depart, departing in peace and to come again when I next call.

That is it.

Allow the small, ritual candle to burn out completely. If you can't burn it safely on the altar, carefully move it to a safe area. I usually use a bathtub or empty fireplace. You could use the center of your stove top or even put the candle in a cold oven, on a cookie sheet, which prevents wax from spilling onto the oven bottom.

    Now, the hardest part; Walk away from the altar and put the issue out of your mind. Trust in the King to deliver, and put doubt out of your mind.

Pathworking the Lust Ritual

As with the standard ritual, please make sure the target of your lust, or love, is actually available or willing to enter into a relationship with you, no matter how brief. This ritual will not attract to you a famous movie star who lives hundreds, or thousands, of miles away. When I tested this ritual, I targeted a well-known actress. To date, she has yet to make contact. And that's as far as I'm willing to test this particular magick.

You will need the smaller Lust/Love sigil along with your petition. You will also need a sterile lancet and a fire-safe bowl for the offering.

When ready, settle yourself in and allow yourself to relax into an alpha state, if you can. Before beginning, just after you've relaxed, protect yourself. The very best way is to surround yourself with golden light. You do this by imagining a golden light starting in your heart center, which spreads out to surround your entire body, out to a few feet. Allow this gold light to solidify, which creates impenetrable energy barrier to any non-beneficial energies you might encounter.

> **Visualize a long hallway, like in an old mansion. The walls are deep red - lit by candles.**
> **At the furthest end is a rose-colored door. Walk to**

this door.

As you near the door, it opens.

You enter a small sitting room. A fire in the fireplace.

Asmodeus is in an armchair by the fire.

He points to another chair. You sit.

Talk to him, and read your petition.

Look into the fire, and visualize your desired outcome.

Thank Asmodeus for his time.

Now, make sure to work the sacrifice. Again, this needs to be a small drop of blood onto the King's small sigil. Burn this, allowing it to burn in the bowl. Make sure it is totally consumed by the fire.

CHAPTER EIGHT

Modifying Any Ritual

I have fielded many, many questions - both via my contact form on my website and through my Facebook page, on changing a ritual.

My rituals are just templates, and are designed for you to alter them in any way you need in order to meet your goals. You can combine "Wrath" with Hell's Banker to cut off competitors while also asking for more and better clients.

When making modifications, feel free to use colors of candles that match your desire. A list of color correspondences is in the appendix.

Things you shouldn't try to change include the blood sacrifices. Stick to using your own blood, do not harm any animals. Asmodeus isn't Sorath.

If you have a specific need not addressed by the rituals in this book, feel free to experiment. Combine a green candle with an orange, and do a ritual to Asmodeus to remove blocks to expanding your income.

You may find that working a series of rituals to Asmodeus would work, such as a King Asmodeus ritual to call in the Progress Jinn, followed by a ritual to the Banker aspect of Asmodeus to open up new wealth channels.

You might find that working a ritual while in an altered mental state to be beneficial. This is accomplished by using any relaxation method to get you into an alpha-state, a semi-awake dreamy state of mind, where it's easier to visualize the desired outcome of a ritual. Instead of waiting until an actual ritual, go into this state and visualize the whole ritual in your mind.

This is especially true when you work a pathworking ritual mentally. Get into a daydream state of mind, and run the pathworking.

CHAPTER NINE

The Sigils

These sigils were given to me by Asmodeus, in his various aspects, then I cleaned up my artwork, so that the sigil is as simple as I can make it.

To activate any sigil, go into a simple ritual, and call Asmodeus using his traditional ENN, and ask him to bless the sigil. Then pass the physical print of the sigil through the incense smoke.

Now, it's ready for use.

Download all of them here:

https://davepsychic.com/asmodeus-sigils-2/

DAVID THOMPSON

Asmodeus Master Sigil

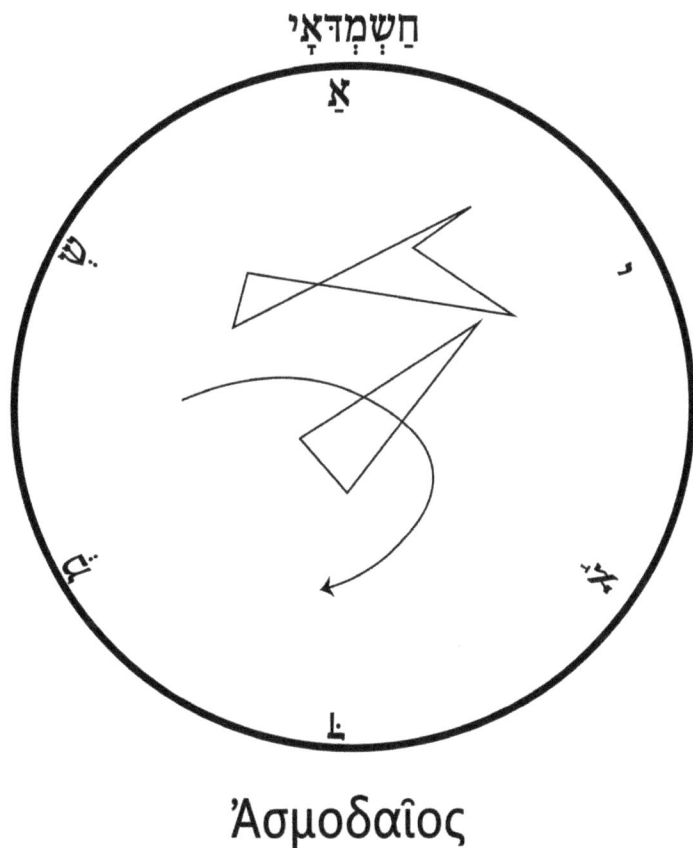

Asmodeus – King of the Daemons

King of the Jinn Master Sigil

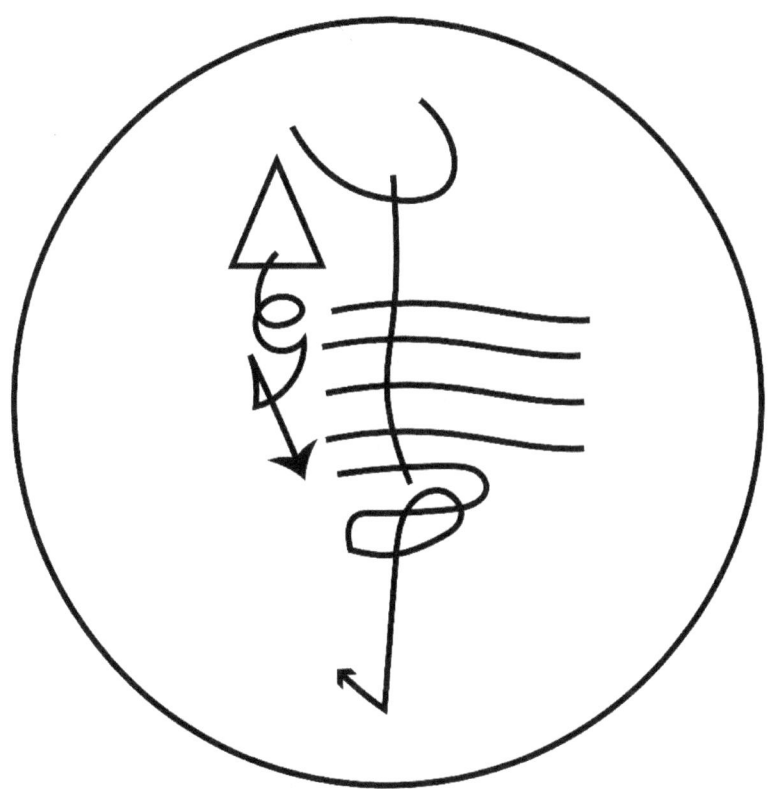

Asmodeus – King of the Daemons

Hell's Banker Sigil

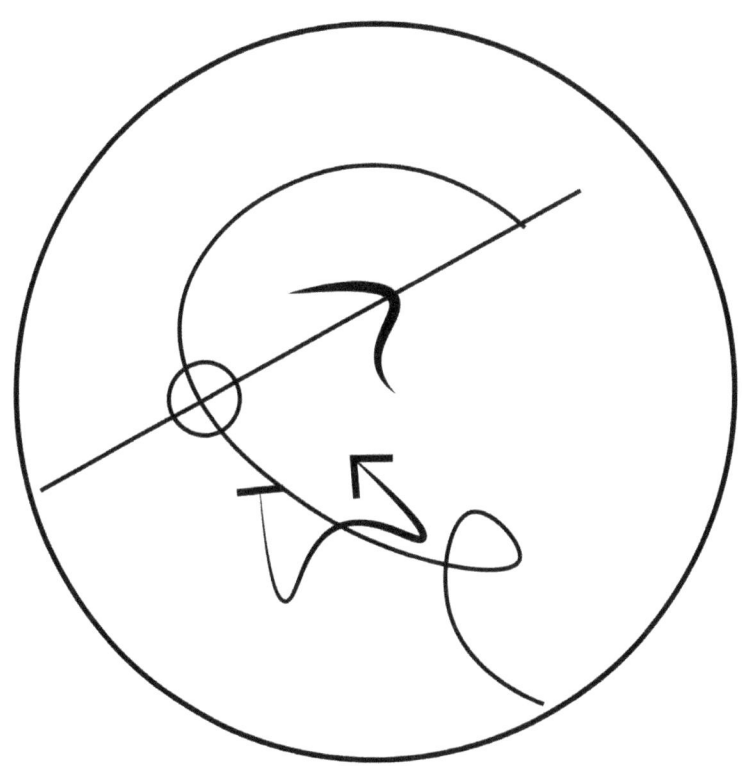

Asmodeus – King of the Daemons

Asmodeus the Wrathful Sigil

Asmodeus – King of the Daemons

King of Lust Sigil

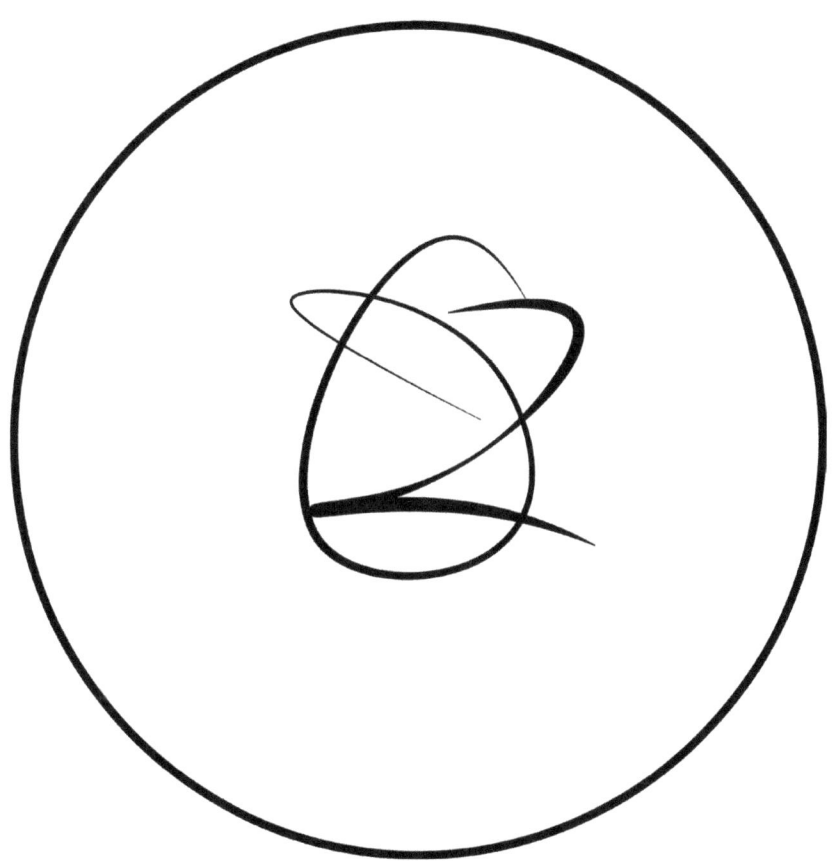

King of Love Sigil

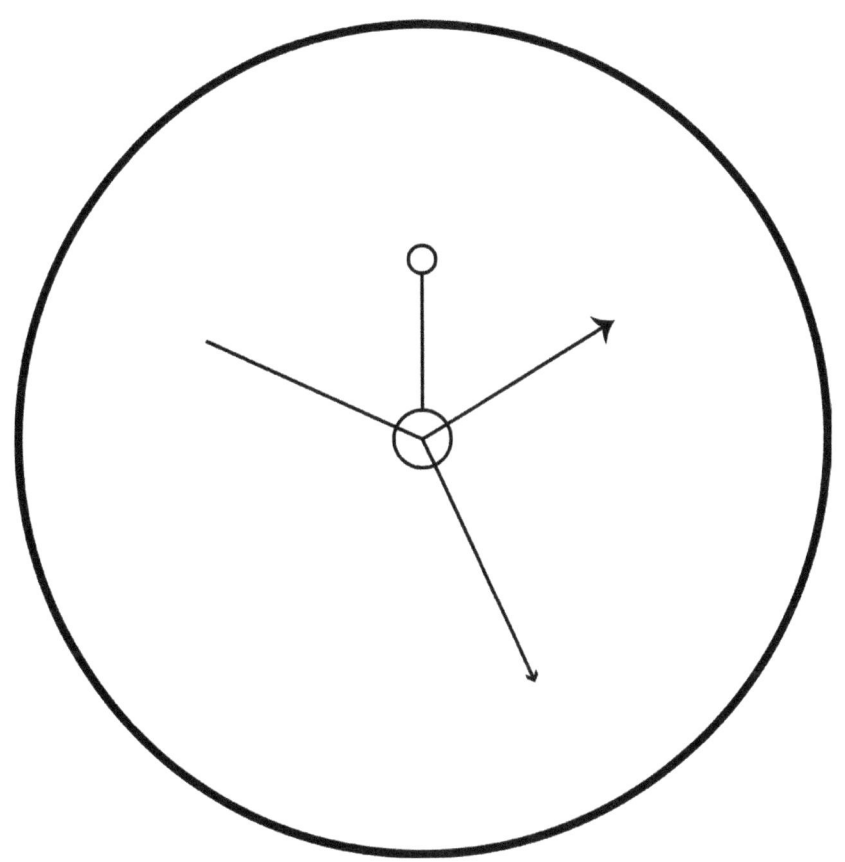

APPENDIX

Recipes

Black Salt for Cursing

To make black salt, two methods, both work.

Method One:

Crush a piece of charcoal. Power the charcoal.

Take 1 tablespoon of coarse salt (pickling or canning salt, no need for fancy salt)

Combine this salt with a teaspoon of the crushed charcoal.

Mix well, and store in a tightly sealed jar.

Method Two:

Chop up some sage, bay leaves and cayenne peppers.

Mix and put into a saucepan you don't mind getting ruined.

(*Be careful with the smoke from this, it'll irritate your eyes and sinuses)

In a well-ventilated area, or outside on a grill, begin cooking the herbs and pepper, and allow it to burn and char. Once it's completely burned, allow it to cool.

Crush the resulting ashes into a powder, and mix with table salt or pickling salt.

The Pendulum

Don't happen to have a Pendulum? No worries! No sense in making this harder than it is. Don't over think. Just make a pendulum!

A pendulum can be made from most anything. All you really need is a length of string or jewelry chain, and something to tie at the bottom.

You can use a ring, a small stone, or even a house key.

Just attach the ring or key to the end of the string or chain, and TA DAH! A pendulum! Wasn't that EASY? Simpler *IS* better!

Activating and Charging your Pendulum

Before working the ritual that uses a pendulum, let's first consecrate the pendulum.

To do this, place the pendulum on your workspace and hold your hands over it.

Imagine a light entering your head and flowing into your hands, then into the pendulum.

Now say:

In the name of EH-EI-EH I ask you, Angel METATRON to bless this pendulum and shape its energies

for spirit communication with Genius entities. Make it safe for myself while I use this pendulum. So be it! Amein! (That last work is Hebraic for So be IT)

Now, your pendulum is ready for use.

Pendulum Charts
Alphabet Chart

Yes/No Chart

Write in your own answers

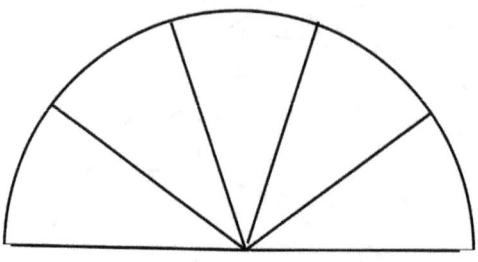

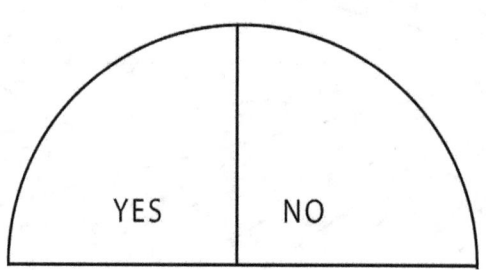

Pendulum Wheel Dates

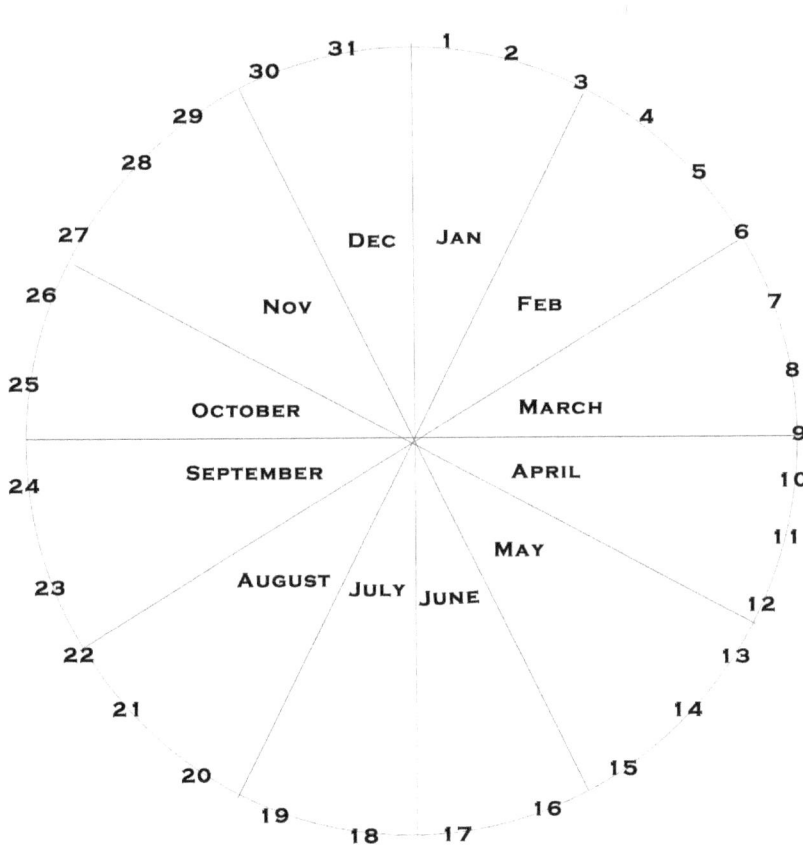

Full size charts available online – see the links.

Suggestions and Links

(The following links are affiliate links for Amazon)

"Power Tarot More Than 100 Spreads That Give Specific Answers to Your Most Important Question Paperback–Illustrated, by Trish Macgregor and Phyllis Vega. Possibly the most useful book on the tarot I have ever read. I have used this book since its publication in 1998. Buy the actual book, as the Kindle is hard to dog ear and bookmark. https://amzn.to/3EWBCZH

Hell's Money - one of the props needed while dealing with Asmodeus in his banker aspect. Most of what you'll find is thin paper, which burns nicely. My recommendation is https://amzn.to/3H2WqBr

Drawing the Pentacle while casting the circle

During the casting of the circle, you are advised to draw a pentacle in the air while facing each compass direction.

I usually begin at the top, and quickly trace the pentacle in the air. Do this a few times, and it'll be easy.

Here's a handy diagram.

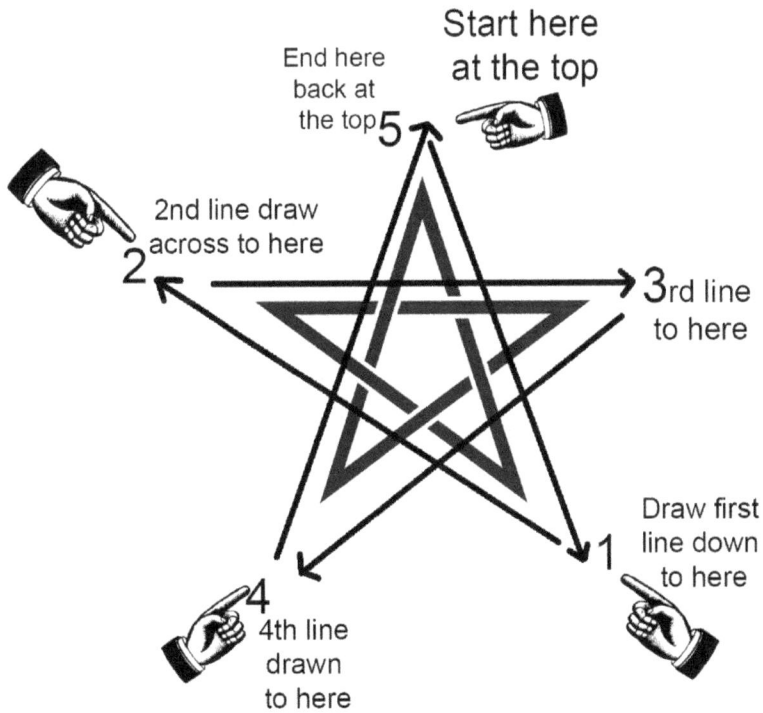

Color Correspondences in Magick

Candle colors and Days:
- Sunday– Gold or yellow candles
- Monday– Silver, Grey or White
- Tuesday-Red
- Wednesday-Purple
- Thursday– Blue
- Friday-Green
- Saturday– Black or Purple

Candle colors and purposes:

- Allergies- Violet
- Anxiety- Rose
- Colds- Green/violet
- Depression-Orange/Indigo/Rose
- Insomnia-Blue
- Indigestion-Yellow
- Fever-Blue
- Headaches-Green/blue
- Diabetes-Yellow

White

- The Goddess
- Higher Self
- Purity
- Peace
- Virginity
- (substitutes any other color)

Black
- Binding
- Shapeshifting
- Protection
- Repels Negativity

Brown
- Special Favors
- To Influence Friendships

Silver
- The Goddess
- Astral energy
- Female energy
- Telepathy
- Clairvoyance
- Intuition
- Dreams

Purple
- Third Eye
- Psychic Ability
- Hidden Knowledge
- To Influence People in High Places
- Spiritual Power

Blue
- Element of Water
- Wisdom
- Protection
- Calm
- Good Fortune
- Opening Blocked Communication
- Spiritual Inspiration

Green
- The Element of Earth
- Physical Healing
- Monetary success
- Mother Earth
- Tree and Plant Magic
- Growth
- Personal Goals

Asmodeus – King of the Daemons

Pink
- Affection
- Romance
- Affection
- Caring
- Nurturing
- Planetary Good Will

Red
- Element of Fire
- Passion
- Strength
- Fast action
- Career Goals
- Lust
- Driving Force
- Survival
- Blood of the Moon

Orange
- General Success
- Property Deals
- Legal matters
- Justice

- Selling

Copper
- Professional Growth
- Business Fertility
- Career Maneuvers
- Passion
- Money Goals

Gold
- The God
- Promote Winning
- Power of the Male
- Happiness

Yellow
- The Element of Air
- Intelligence
- The Sun
- Memory
- Logical Imagination
- To Accelerate Learning
- To Break Mental Blocks

About the Author

Dave is an author of adult fantasy (The Furies series) as well as author of occult books about magick.

David began working ritual magick back in the 1970s. He took a brief break, then used the power of this magick to create a photography career which took him to Los Angeles and work as a photographer for multiple magazines.

David has studied magick in all forms, and in 2018, released a three-part magick instruction course in High Magick. Thousands of students have benefited from David's unique teaching style, making ceremonial magick accessible to everyone.

This book on Asmodeus is book 7 in his High Magick Series.

Dave also has a series on Grecian Magick, exploring the aspects of ceremonial magick with the gods and goddesses of ancient Greece.

Dave's Facebook Page:
https://www.facebook.com/DavePsychic/

Secrets of Magick Facebook Group:
https://www.facebook.com/groups/secretsofmagick

Join the Grecian Magick Facebook group!
https://www.facebook.com/groups/grecianmagick

And finally, Dave's webpage, book readings and his services:
https://davepsychic.com

Sign-up for my Newsletter and get a FREE E-Book!
https://davepsychic.com/newsletter

Magick Books by David Thompson

Available as EPUB, Paperback and Hardcover (*)

High Magick Series
- High Magick 101
- Daemons of High Magick
- Daemons and the Law of Attraction(*)
- Magick of Astaroth(*)
- Lilith: Goddess of Darkness and Light (*)
- Daemons of Fortune(*)

Grecian Magick Series
- Magick of Apollo
- Magick of Hermes

- Magick of Aphrodite
- Magick of Fortuna*
- Greco-Roman Wealth Magick*
- Magick of the Sirens/Magick of the Muses

Fiction Novels by David Thompson

The Furies Series

- Angels of Vengeance
- Descent into Tartarus
- Furies: Beginnings
- Brianna: Making of a Fury

www.ingramcontent.com/pod-product-compliance
Lightning Source LLC
LaVergne TN
LVHW020434070526
838199LV00031B/624/J